DECORATING
with HERBS

Decorating
with Herbs

Simon Lycett

Photography by Michelle Garrett

Reader's Digest

The Reader's Digest Association, Inc.
Pleasantville, New York/Montreal

A READER'S DIGEST BOOK

Conceived, edited and designed by
Susan Berry for Collins & Brown Limited

Copyright © Collins & Brown Limited 1998
Text copyright © Simon Lycett 1998
Illustrations copyright © Collins & Brown Limited 1998

Project Editor Ginny Surtees
Editors Alison Freegard and Amanda Lebentz
Designer Sue Metcalfe-Megginson
Managing Art Editor Kevin Williams
Art Director Roger Bristow
Illustrations Clare Roberts

International Standard Book Number: 0-7621-0126-1

Library of Congress Cataloging in Publication Data has been applied for.

Reader's Digest and the Pegasus logo are registered
trademarks of The Reader's Digest Association, Inc.

Printed and bound in Hong Kong

CONTENTS

INTRODUCTION

ONE OF MY most vivid childhood memories is of the lavender hedge which grew at the bottom of my grandmother's garden. A great plantswoman and talented school principal, she encouraged my interest in plants, flowers, and herbs. It was at her knee that I learned my multiplication table, and, of far more interest to me, how to make lavender bags, those beautiful little sachets of dried and seemingly dead flower heads which scented the air and all that they touched.

I have never lost my childhood enthusiasm for herbs. As an adult, seeing the first boxes of English lavender arrive at my local flower market never fails to thrill me. But, rather than reserve herbs merely for the kitchen, I strive to use them, either fresh or dried, as much as possible in my decorations and throughout the home. Their gentle perfume has a dimension and appeal lacking in so many of the more mundane florist's flowers that have been overbred and processed.

This interest in the versatility of herbs, not just as medicinal or culinary ingredients, but as decorative items, is nothing new. The Egyptians were extravagant users of herbs and flowers for decorative purposes and they grew and recorded over 500 herbs. There is also some evidence of a Chinese herbal being written during the third millennium B.C. The first complete herbal, the *Materia Medica* was written by Dioscorides, a Greek, in the first century after Christ, and was regarded as a major reference work for thousands of years. From the ninth century A.D., knowledge of herbs came to Europe via the Arab occupation of Spain, and as civilizations grew and communities

Scented flower water, traditionally used as a refreshing face wash, looks wonderful stored in glass or opaque bottles on a bathroom windowsill.

6

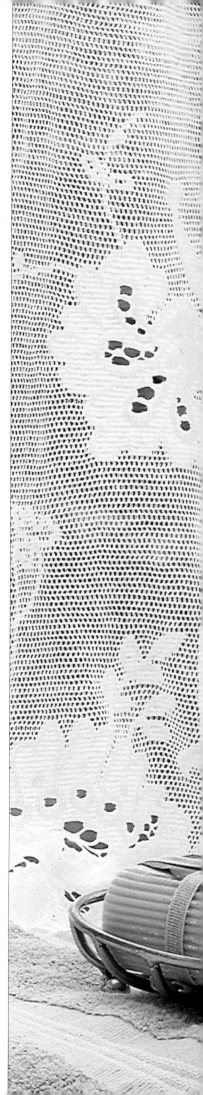

developed, small plots of land were created close to the wealthier dwellings for use as gardens in which fruits, vegetables and, most importantly, herbs were grown.

In medieval times, religious establishments played a major role in developing the cultivation of herbs. Most monastery gardens supplied their local churches with cut flowers for decoration and the apothecary with the herbs he needed to prepare potions, ointments and waters for the sick.

Early in the 1500s two English herbals were produced: *Banckes's Herbal* in 1525 and *The Grete Herbal* in 1526. Later in the century, during the reign of Elizabeth 1, the herb garden really came into its own

and the preparation of the herbs was a chief task for the woman of the house, who would have been paramedic, midwife and mother, as well as cook and housekeeper. Primarily used as treatments for various wounds and illnesses, bunches of scented herbs were also hung up around the house to freshen the air and leaves and petals were scattered on the ground to mask the unsavory stenches of day-to-day life.

The aristocratic Elizabethan home would have had a "still room", where herbs and flowers were prepared, stored, and dried, and a distillery used to extract the essential oils from plants grown in the garden. Today we have a rich heritage of perfumes, infusions,

Rosemary pomanders are versatile decorations—use fresh or dried to scent the air and provide interest with their sculptural forms.

Votive candles look charming in jars wrapped with bay leaves and secured with decorative yarn or twine.

potpourris, herbal pillows, tussie-mussies, and lavender bags, all of which were familiar sights in the Elizabethan still rooms. It is an enchanting thought in this day and age, that we are able to enjoy the scents and sights of long ago, with the satisfaction of knowing that we have made the herb decorations ourselves.

Herbs and spices are rewarding to work with because of their varied fragrances, colors, textures, shapes, and forms. Imagine how much more interesting and attractive a simple vase of roses would look if a few stems of fragrant bay and rosemary were added in place of unscented and uninspired florist's greenery. Envisage relaxing in a hot bath as fragrant as a cup of peppermint tea, or washing with soap scented with rosemary and thyme, prior to reclining on pillows filled with fragrant, sleep-inducing herbs and flowers.

This book guides you through a variety of projects, tailored for different areas of the home, using fresh or dried herbs and spices as the primary ingredients. Recipes give an indication of quantities needed, as well as combinations which have been tried and tested. These are offered merely as suggestions, in the hope that you will be inspired and experiment with your own projects and recipes. You may well come to think of herbs in the same way that I do—as essential ingredients for making life more special.

Tuck these pretty gingham lavender bags into linen so their gentle perfume lingers on fresh sheets and pillowcases.

Candles wrapped in thyme look good on a table set for dinner; the warmed herbs also exude a soothing fragrance.

Herbs for the Table

Herbs are used to enhance the flavor of food in many different ways. They can also be introduced to the table as decorations—this guarantees a memorable dining experience. Herb-filled napkin rings and tray cloths make fragrant and original place settings, while flowering pots, table centerpieces, and festive winter arrangements bring a bare tabletop to life—your guests are sure to want to come back for more.

HERB NAPKIN RINGS

Unusual, but simple to make, these napkin rings last for several years. They are also wonderful to give as presents, especially if you include lovely antique damask or simple white linen napkins rolled up inside.

ONE OF MY FAVORITE tips when entertaining is to use traditional, starched, white damask napkins—the larger and more heavily starched they are, the better. I collect them from flea markets because I prefer the feel and character of old linen. By rolling them within these herb-filled rings, you allow the fragrance of the herbs to gently permeate the fabric. For the napkin ring fabric, I have used a natural, coarsely woven, linen-type material, but any fabric that allows the natural herb aromas to filter through will do—it might be fun to use a fabric that matches your tablecloth or dining-room curtains. Almost any combination of herbs and spices would work, but it is sensible to keep lavender and roses to a minimum because the heady scents can be overpowering near food.

HERBS AND SPICES USED

To fill approximately six napkin rings:

1oz (30g) dried thyme	2 sprigs fresh mint, or
1oz (30g) dried mint	3 fresh bay leaves
1oz (30g) dried chamomile	3 sticks fresh lemon grass
3 dried bay leaves	
1oz (30g) dried rosemary	*To decorate:*
2oz (55g) cinnamon sticks	6 sprigs fresh rosemary

MAKING THE NAPKIN RINGS

For six napkin rings you will need: twelve 6in (15cm) long, 2in (5cm) wide strips of open-weave fabric; needle and thread; cotton cord; scissors; ceramic bowl, for mixing herbs; and fresh sprigs of rosemary, bay, or thyme, for decoration.

Use two lengths of material sewn together to form a tube, with one end folded and stitched, which is then filled with herbs. A good basic recipe uses dried thyme, mint, chamomile, and cinnamon pieces. Mix these thoroughly in a ceramic bowl first, adding additional herbs if you wish.

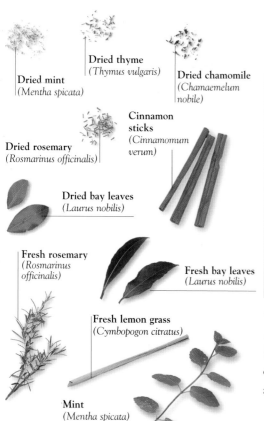

Dried thyme
(Thymus vulgaris)

Dried mint
(Mentha spicata)

Dried chamomile
(Chamaemelum nobile)

Cinnamon sticks
(Cinnamomum verum)

Dried rosemary
(Rosmarinus officinalis)

Dried bay leaves
(Laurus nobilis)

Fresh rosemary
(Rosmarinus officinalis)

Fresh bay leaves
(Laurus nobilis)

Fresh lemon grass
(Cymbopogon citratus)

Mint
(Mentha spicata)

1 Make tubes for the herbs by stitching together the longest edges of two 6in (15cm) lengths of fabric. Neatly fold over one end twice, by ½in (12mm), pin, and stitch to close. Turn right sides out.

2 Fill each tube with well-mixed dried herbs and cinnamon. Be careful not to overfill them or it will be difficult to insert the napkin. Add the sprig of rosemary, the mint or bay leaves, and fresh lemon grass.

5 Roll or loosely fold each napkin, and pull it through the ring. Tie the cotton cord around the center of the ring and make a neat bow. Add a sprig of fresh rosemary or a couple of sticks of lemon grass to decorate.

3 Check that the tubes are of the same length so the ring sizes will be the same. Trim off any excess fabric from the open end, make a couple of neat folds, and stitch to close.

4 Bring the ends of the tube together to form the ring, then pin carefully, making sure the sides and side seam correspond. Stitch the ends together neatly.

HERB TRAY CLOTH

More decorative than purely practical, this elegant cloth has been filled with fragrant dried herbs, which release
their delicate scents when a warm plate or cup is placed on them. Adding dried marigold petals
to the contents brightens the cloth and continues the color theme of the tray setting.

THE WORKBENCH AT my studio is often littered with dried herb stems, discarded as I work on decorations or floral arrangements. When I placed a hot cup of coffee on these materials I noticed that their fragrance was released by the heat. I was inspired to reproduce this effect in a more manageable and practical way, so I designed this tray cloth. I chose a simple linen placemat as the base material, but you can use damask for a more sumptuous effect or another material of your choice.

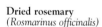

HERBS USED

For each tray cloth:
2oz (55g) dried marigold petals
2oz (55g) dried tarragon
2oz (55g) dried rosemary

Dried tarragon
(*Artemisia dracunculus*)

Dried marigold
(*Tagetes patula*)

Dried rosemary
(*Rosmarinus officinalis*)

MAKING THE HERB TRAY CLOTH

In addition to the herbs, you will need: linen or damask placemat, measuring approximately 18in by 12in (45cm by 30cm); lightweight fabric, such as organza or cotton, 18in by 11in (40cm by 28cm); sewing machine; handful of pins; needle; and thread.

Machine-stitch the lightweight fabric onto the base cloth and leave an opening to fill the sachet with herbs. Lay the cloth on a flat surface and fill the sachet by hand or with a spoon, spreading the herbs out as evenly as possible. Pin the opening closed and carefully pin across the sachet, from left to right, in straight lines approximately 1in (2.5cm) apart, to form columns. Repeat this process from top to bottom to create a pinned grid—this keeps the herbs in place. Machine-stitching in a freestyle pattern means you do not have to worry about sewing in straight lines and you can sew in between the pins. If you are an experienced sewer, stitch along the pins for a neat, symmetrical look.

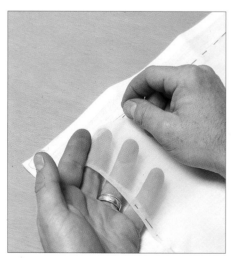

1 Pin the lightweight fabric onto the center of the base cloth. Make sure that the rough edges of the lightweight fabric are pinned under (it may help to iron the edges under before you begin).

2 Sew along the two short sides, one of the long sides, and two-thirds of the remaining side with a zigzag stitch. Leave an opening to fill the sachet with the dried herbs.

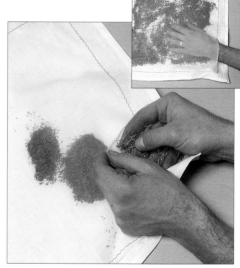

3 On a flat surface, carefully fill the sachet with the herbs. Spread them out evenly, thinly covering the whole area. Pin the opening closed, being careful not to trap any herbs.

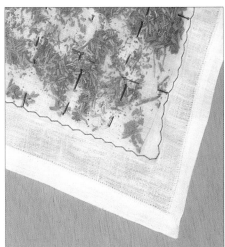

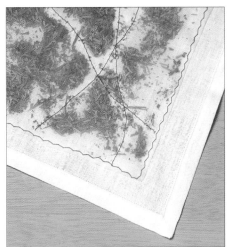

4 Divide the sachet into a grid using pins (see Making the Herb Tray Cloth, opposite) to hold the herbs evenly in each of the squares. Using zigzag stitch, close the pinned opening.

5 With the sewing machine set to a short straight stitch, quilt all over the sachet, beginning in one corner and being careful not to run over the pins as you sew. You can also stitch by hand.

What could be more welcoming than being served a delicious breakfast on a tray or table laid with such an original and fragrant cloth? These elegant linen mats are also ideal for the dinner table, as they not only look colorful and fresh, but also smell marvelous as each releases its individual fragrance when a warmed dinner plate is placed on it.

FLOWERING POTS

Any fancy or plain containers, or terracotta pots, as long as they are of roughly the same style, can be used for paired groups of attractive flowering herbs. You can also include some of the more unusual "salad" herbs, such as marigolds or clary sage.

RESHLY CUT HERBS planted in pots make a much appreciated, thoughtful, yet inexpensive, gift. As an avid flea market and thrift store browser, I often pick up "one-of-a-kind" flowerpots at bargain prices. Planting or arranging herbs in them seems much more stylish than presenting the empty pots as gifts (that is, if I can bring myself to part with the pots at all). Use freshly cut herbs, arranging them as a florist would arrange fresh flowers (see below), and the herbs can slowly dry out "in situ," making an equally long-lasting display. Make sure that any cut herbs have stems strong enough to support the flower heads while they dry in this upright position.

MAKING THE FLOWERING POTS

You will need: suitable containers; chicken wire cut into 6in (15cm) square pieces, for each 8in (20cm) diameter pot; stub wires or florist's tape to keep the chicken wire in place; and dry moss. First, line each container with a thin layer of dry moss and then follow the instructions for the lavender pots, shown below. The safflower pots are made in exactly the same way.

HERBS USED
For each 8in (20cm) diameter pot:
60 stems lavender
40 stems safflower

Safflower
(Carthamus tinctorius)

Lavender
(Lavandula angustifolia)

1 Crumple the chicken wire into a ball and push it into the container so it sits just below the lip. Secure with stub wires or florist's tape and fill in any gaps with moss.

2 Working from one side of the container, take a few sprigs of the herb and arrange them in the wire. The goal is to make the herbs appear to be growing naturally.

Lavender and safflower make a bold, contrastingly colored display and are ideal for this treatment because they dry out slowly, retaining their color and shape.

3 Turning the container, add enough herbs to fill the pot. The chicken wire will act as a support for the herbs.

4 When the arrangement is as full as desired, fill the edges with moss and fill in holes with an extra sprig or two.

TABLE
CENTERPIECE

This wonderfully aromatic basket of fresh culinary herbs is practical as well as decorative—the herbs can be selected to complement a soup, pasta, or salad. Family and guests can pick a couple of leaves or a sprig of herb to flavor their meal.

THIS TABLE ARRANGEMENT is quick and simple to make, and requires little in the way of equipment or expertise. Almost any culinary herb can be substituted for the ones shown here, and they can either be picked fresh from the garden or bought in their own soil-filled containers. Choose herbs that make a good decorative contrast and also complement your meal. Parsley is a good choice because it makes a great addition to many dishes. Basil is a delicious accompaniment to salads and pasta dishes, and if you opt for the purple-leaved variety, will add a bold splash of color. Use sage—with great discretion— to flavor cream cheese. Mint (or chervil and dill) is excellent for freshening the palate between courses. Of the various mints, apple and spearmint both have an excellent flavor. Be careful with rue—it has poisonous qualities and is used purely decoratively to add texture and display its beautiful silvery foliage. Be sure to warn diners not to use the rue.

HERBS USED
To fill each pot in the basket: (8-12 sprigs) of mint, parsley, sage, and thyme

To decorate the basket: 30-50 stems of fresh rosemary, each about 10in (24cm) long

Arrange the herbs so their different textures, colors, and leaf shapes contrast with one another to make them look as appetizing as possible.

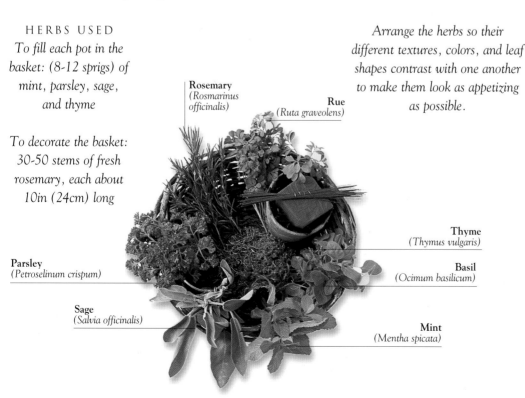

Rosemary
(Rosmarinus officinalis)

Rue
(Ruta graveolens)

Thyme
(Thymus vulgaris)

Parsley
(Petroselinum crispum)

Basil
(Ocimum basilicum)

Sage
(Salvia officinalis)

Mint
(Mentha spicata)

MAKING THE TABLE CENTERPIECE

You will need: one round, open-weave basket, 12in (30cm) diameter, 3-4in (8-10cm) deep; moss; florist's medium-gauge stub wires, 6in (15cm) long, bent double into "hairpins;" selection of terracotta pots, 2-3in (5-8cm) diameter; black plastic (such as a garbage bag), cut to line the terracotta pots; presoaked florist's foam, cut to fit the pots.

The basket needs to be fairly open-weave but it doesn't really matter what it looks like because its sides will be completely covered. Even older-looking pots with chipped rims are usable. If you already have potted herbs, just transfer these directly into the terracotta pots to create the arrangement.

1 To cover the basket with the rosemary stems, hold 10-12 stems at a time against the side of the basket, cut ends protruding slightly below the bottom. Place a wire "hairpin" around the rosemary stems and secure by pushing the ends through to the inside of the basket. Twist them tightly and press flat.

2 Continue to add the bunches of rosemary around the basket, working in one direction and attaching all the wires at the same level. Make sure the tips of the foliage are more or less level, 1in (2.5cm) above the basket edge. Trim the stem ends flush with the base of the basket, so it sits level.

4 Arrange the pots in the basket, placing the tallest in the center or to the back of the arrangement. If necessary, add extra moss to ensure the pots are packed close together so they stay in an almost upright position.

5 Taking one type of cut herb per pot, insert several stems into the florist's foam to look as if they are growing naturally. Make sure the florist's foam and liners are hidden, while the terracotta pots remain visible.

3 Half-fill the basket with moss. If you are using cut herbs, line the pots with plastic and place cut pieces of presoaked florist's foam inside, protruding slightly above the rim. To create visual interest in the finished arrangement, vary the height by stacking some of the pots, one within another, before you add the florist's foam.

Edible Table Centerpiece

This scaled-down table arrangement is made up entirely of edible herbs. Easy to create, it has the added attraction of including freshly chopped herbs, in the terracotta pot, available to season the food. A versatile and colorful display, it is perfect for a wide range of occasions, from a summer lunch to an intimate dinner, or even for a large party—place individual arrangements in front of each setting. To assemble this centerpiece, start with the same method shown opposite. Cover a small basket, approximately 6-8in (15-20cm) in diameter, with 30 sprigs of rosemary. Cut a piece of presoaked florist's foam to fit inside the basket at half its depth. Wedge the bottom of the terracotta pot into the center of the florist's foam and insert about 20 sprigs of parsley into the exposed foam to form a collar around the pot, 1in (2cm) from its rim. Fill the pot with freshly chopped herbs.

6 Before you place the arrangement, stand back and look at the centerpiece to see if any gaps need filling. Make any necessary adjustments to the pots to create a balanced display. Finally, mist the herbs lightly with water.

Created from rosemary and parsley, this edible centerpiece is a fun and original way to decorate a table laid for an al fresco lunch. The rich greens of the fresh herbs add a splash of color to the simple, informal setting.

21

FESTIVE WINTER TABLE

Illuminated by flickering candlelight, neatly trimmed rosemary, cloves, eucalyptus,
and bright safflowers make up a stunning table centerpiece, which
will bring cheer to any winter celebration.

ALTHOUGH MANY OF us tend to think of herbs as summer plants, there are a wide range of evergreen herbs that survive through winter and provide us with ample material for cutting and using indoors. One of the most useful is rosemary, which can be grown in even the smallest garden or windowbox.

This beautiful table decoration is ideal for a winter dinner party, bringing welcome natural greenery and flower color to the table. Here, rosemary is combined with cloves, another seasonal favorite, to recreate a stylized "knot garden," in which the rosemary symbolizes low clipped boxwood hedging and the cloves resemble gravel. As an alternative to cloves, crushed dried lemon balm or sage would also smell good and create a similar effect.

For the corners of the centerpiece, safflower heads are teamed with ghostly gray-blue eucalyptus in terracotta pots. Eucalyptus is another year-round plant which is longlasting, dries well, and smells wonderful. The pots may be used in conjunction with the rosemary "hedge," or look just as good when displayed on their own in pairs, as a small group or individually. *Caution:* Never leave lit candles unattended, and you should keep a close eye on these candles so they do not burn down too close to the herbs.

HERBS AND SPICES USED
For the centerpiece: 200 sprigs rosemary,
9oz (250g) cloves. For each pot:
1 sprig eucalyptus, 12 flower heads safflower

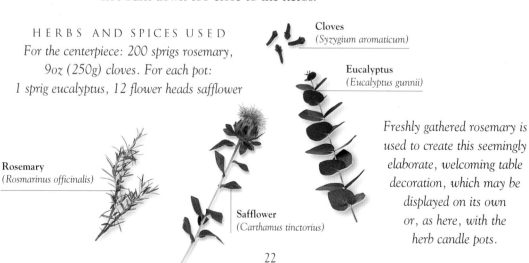

Cloves
(Syzygium aromaticum)

Eucalyptus
(Eucalyptus gunnii)

Rosemary
(Rosmarinus officinalis)

Safflower
(Carthamus tinctorius)

Freshly gathered rosemary is used to create this seemingly elaborate, welcoming table decoration, which may be displayed on its own or, as here, with the herb candle pots.

22

MAKING THE FESTIVE WINTER CENTERPIECE

You will need: large block of florist's foam, approximately 18in (45cm) long, 12in (30cm) wide, and 4in (10cm) deep; saucer; sharp knife; scissors; 4 terracotta pots; 4 blocks florist's foam to fit in each pot; 4 candles, approximately 6in (15cm) tall and 2in (5cm) diameter; 12 split canes, 3in (8cm) long; florist's tape; sheet of plastic.

If the block of foam does not exactly fit the above measurements, you can always cut a larger block to size, or you may want to cut the rectangle into a square to suit the shape of your table. Adding the rosemary will increase the overall size by 2in (5cm) in each direction. Before you start, break the rosemary into 4-5in (10-12cm) sprigs, snapping just above a leaf joint to avoid any twiggy ends being visible.

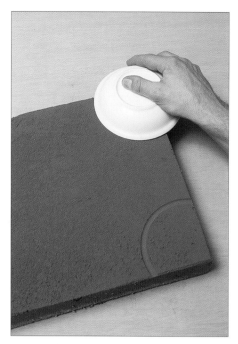

1 Gently press an inverted saucer or bowl into each corner of the florist's foam block, leaving a slight indentation.

2 Using a sharp knife, cut out the four marked semicircles. You may find it easier to make a series of incisions into the foam, cutting down toward the base. It does not matter if the edges are untidy, as they will be concealed by the herbs.

4 Line each terracotta pot with a piece of plastic and press the soaked florist's foam into each so it protrudes just above the rim. Using florist's tape, attach three split canes around the base of the candle to form a tripod. Push the tripod into the center of the foam and make sure the candle is straight.

5 Disguise the taped base of the candle by pushing eucalyptus sprigs into the foam, forming a collar around the bottom of each candle. Cut the safflower into short flower-topped stems and push several into the foam, filling any gaps.

Scented-leaved Geranium Pot

As a variation to eucalyptus leaves and safflowers, herb candle pots can be made from bunches of scented geraniums, which although not frost-hardy, may survive mild winters. Grown for their perfumed and often patterned leaves, cultivated varieties of this southern African herb have been favorites in Europe for centuries. You could also mix different herbs together in one pot, and this is an ideal way to use up those odd sprigs of herbs from the garden that have managed to survive the winter.

3 Push the short pieces of rosemary into the top edge and sides of the foam at a slight angle. Continue around the sides of the foam until it is completely covered. Using a pair of sharp scissors, trim the rosemary back, leaving about 2in (5cm) on top and 1in (3cm) along the sides to create a trimmed appearance. Cover the bare top with cloves.

6 When all four pots are complete, place them at each corner of the rosemary- and clove-filled tray. Make sure that the candles do not burn too close to the herb collars.

Beneath the warmth of a burning candle, scented geranium leaves release a sweet and subtle fragrance. A cream candle coordinates perfectly with the pretty cream and green variegated foliage.

Decorative Accents

The beauty of herbs and spices is that they are so versatile—in addition to their many practical and fragrant uses, they can also look breathtaking as decorations in their own right. Slender stems of lemon grass look wonderful wrapped around glasses, glossy bay leaves create an impressive topiary, and the textures and colors of a variety of herbs are used to great effect in a garlanded basket, tussie-mussie, and kitchen wall hanging.

HERB-WRAPPED GLASSES

Lemon grass and rosemary are particularly adaptable herbs for decorations because they are sturdy and grow to a good height. Here, each herb is bound around a simple glass tumbler, creating an unusual and fragrant container for pens and paper or for using as a small vase.

WHEN I SEE LEMON GRASS, it always amazes me that it should smell so strongly of the yellow citrus fruit we all know so well, when it bears no resemblance to either the fruit or the tree. However, it has a zingy, fresh fragrance, with a delicate green and parchment appearance, which is so subtle, and the herb needs to be seen close up to be fully appreciated. This project does just that.

As the perfect gift for an avid cook, fill a herb-wrapped glass with a small bouquet of fresh herbs, perhaps cut from your own garden. Filled up with water and placed on the kitchen windowsill, the ingredients for many delicious meals will be close at hand.

Try to select the longest and thickest sticks of fresh lemon grass for your herb tumbler edging, and use a sharp knife to cut them. Pick a straight-sided, short glass—if you have one with a chipped edge or crack, this is a good way to recycle it. When touching lemon grass, you may notice white powder on your hands—this is the drying sap of the lemon grass, which is harmless and will wash off easily. You could also use rosemary for this project, it works just as well, producing a green, bushy effect.

MAKING THE HERB-WRAPPED GLASSES

For each glass (the one shown is 6in (14cm) tall and 3in (7cm) in diameter), you will need: a small, sharp knife; cutting board; ball of twine; and scissors.

As the lemon grass dries out, it will shrink a little, which may cause the stems to become loose. To avoid this, pack the stems tightly together, or use twine in two places, near the top and the bottom of the glass, which will give the glass a slightly different finished look. If using rosemary, you will need approximately 12-15 sprigs per glass (the one shown right is 3in (8cm) tall, 2.5in (7cm) in diameter).

Lemon grass
(*Cymbopogon citratus*)

HERBS USED
For each glass: approximately 20 sticks of lemon grass

1 Use the knife to slice the thickest sticks in half lengthwise. Slender stems can be used whole.

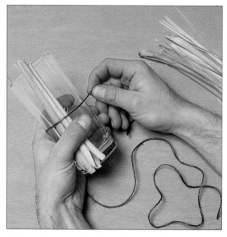

2 Using twine, bind a few stems of grass to the glass by wrapping the twine around them and the glass.

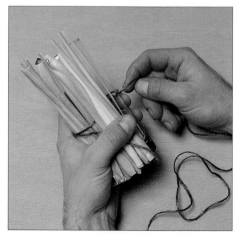

3 Continue to add the lemon grass (6-7 stems at a time), binding them to the glass with the twine as you work.

4 When the glass is completely covered, wind the twine around the middle of the lemon grass several times. Pull the twine as tight as possible and then tie off in a knot.

5 Trim the ends of the stems around the bottom of the glass so the arrangement stands level. Then snip off the ends around the top of the glass.

As well as making attractive desktop containers for stationery, pens, and pencils, these lemon grass- and rosemary-wrapped glasses exude a soothing fragrance as you work.

29

BAY TOPIARY

These little trees have an attractive sculptural quality.

When creating topiary, use glossy, evergreen leaves, such as bay,

for a very simple but contemporary effect.

OR THIS LITTLE topiary "tree" I have used a sphere as my base shape, but square-based pyramids, cubes, or even obelisks are just as effective. Herb topiaries are inexpensive to make, do not need any maintenance or regular pruning like real topiary does, and they look striking, adding an element of the architectural to the home. I particularly like the strong, sleek appearance of bay leaves, and the interesting design shown here is achieved by overlapping the bay leaves in even rows.

It is important that the pot, pole, and sphere make a balanced shape. Too big an sphere and the topiary will look top-heavy; too small a sphere and it will lack impact. As a rough guide, the diameter of the sphere should be similar to the diameter of the top of the pot, and the pole should be roughly as long as the depth of the pot, and that of the sphere (adapt the measurements given right as you wish).

These "trees" are decorative and fragrant and make wonderful presents. They are most attractive when displayed in pairs or in a group—a whole row of bay spheres, pyramids, and obelisks along the center of a dining table, for example, looks very impressive.

MAKING THE BAY TOPIARY

You will need: 5in (12cm) diameter florist's foam sphere; a small quantity of plaster of paris, for securing the pole in the pot; silver birch branch or a similar pole, 7-8in (18-20cm) long and 1in (2.5cm) in diameter; terracotta pot or other container, 4in (10cm) in diameter; glue; medium-gauge florist's wire, cut and bent into 3/4in (2cm) long "hairpins;" small quantity of gravel; and clear varnish spray (optional). The plaster mix should have the consistency of light cream, and will set very quickly in approximately 5 minutes. Insert a few slivers of dried florist's foam into the pot before you pour in the plaster—this will prevent the pot from cracking (plaster expands when it sets).

Bay
(Laurus nobilis)

HERBS USED
Approximately 50 bay leaves of various sizes

1 Fill the pot with plaster of paris mix and position the birch pole firmly in the center, making sure it is upright and stable. Put the pot to one side until the plaster is dry.

2 When the plaster has set, push the sphere gently onto the pole to half the depth of sphere so it fits snugly. Remove the sphere, apply glue to the top of the pole, and then replace it.

3 Working from the top, make the first circle of leaves, choosing the smallest. Wire each leaf with a "hairpin" (see p. 101), wired through the top point of the leaf, then push the wire into the foam to secure the leaf. Overlap the leaves to hide the pins. Work in circles down the sphere, but anchor the leaves at the bottom. For the last ring, glue on half leaves, butting the cut edges against the pole.

4 Finish the arrangement by covering the plaster base with a shallow layer of gravel. Spray the topiary ball with clear varnish so the leaves last longer and have a nice sheen.

The size of this herb topiary makes it ideal for a corner cupboard or shelf. Here it is displayed with a rosemary pomander (see p. 46) and a basket of sage leaves.

HERB-GARLANDED BASKET

Embellished with sprays of dried herbs and seed heads, this decorated basket is perfect

for displaying fruit, potpourri, and pomanders, for storing soap or hand towels

in the bathroom, or for stacks of table linen in the dining room.

OR THIS decorative basket, you can use any flowering or foliage herbs, fresh or dry, since the types and quantities needed are flexible. Herbs grown at home are ideal—harvest them as they reach their peak and hang them up in a cool, airy place to dry. For this basket, I have used one of my favorite seed heads, *Nigella damascena*, or love-in-a-mist, as it is commonly known. It has a pretty shape and its purple-blue stripes echo the color of the lavender. An alternative idea would be to use edible herbs. Create a base with green foliage, such as parsley, bay, and chives, and accent this with lemon grass, garlic, and chilies.

It is important when planning your decoration to use plants with a variety of shapes, textures, colors, and scents. As soon as something begins to look worn out, it can easily be replaced with a fresh spray, perhaps of a different herb.

On a different scale, you can decorate a really large, deep, square log basket with lavender, sage, and bay leaves, and other fragrant herbs. If the basket is filled with logs and placed near the warmth of a fire, the herbs and wood inside will release their wonderful scents into the room.

You will need a basket made of willow or other wood with a similar weave, but it can be of any shape. I prefer a square or rectangular one, with a handle, with sides approximately 12in (30cm) long. You can modify the instructions to suit a special basket—including ones with circular or oval shapes.

This richly decorated basket, in mauves, greens, and golds, can be used to add a touch of glamour to a summer picnic—the contents covered with a starched linen napkin, and a bunch of lavender as the finishing touch.

HERBS USED

For the basket shown, 4 sprays
each of the following dried herbs:
20 love-in-a-mist seed heads,
wired 3 or 5 to a spray
20 sprigs of yarrow, wired
4 or 5 to a spray
20 sprigs of lady's mantle,
wired 4 or 5 to a spray
20 sprigs of lavender, wired 5
to a spray, leaving stems long
20 sprigs of safflower,
wired 4 or 5 to a spray

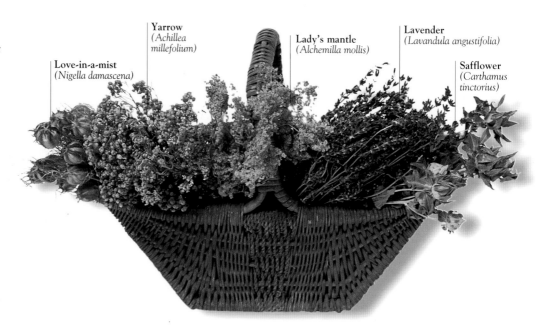

Yarrow
(*Achillea millefolium*)

Lady's mantle
(*Alchemilla mollis*)

Lavender
(*Lavandula angustifolia*)

Love-in-a-mist
(*Nigella damascena*)

Safflower
(*Carthamus tinctorius*)

MAKING THE HERB-GARLANDED BASKET

You will need: a suitable basket; enough thoroughly dried moss or hay for the garland; reel wire; 20-gauge stub wires; raffia or twine to hide the stubs (optional); and a pair of sharp scissors.

Before you begin to decorate the basket, measure a length of reel wire to fit its circumference, plus enough to twist together and secure the ends. This is the base onto which the moss or hay garland for the basket rim will be attached. You will need a second length of wire to use as binding to secure the moss to the base.

Remember to tease the moss to remove any lumps or twiggy pieces. When you attach the garland to the basket rim with the stub wires, it must be secured firmly because the rim supports the sprays of flowers and herbs. The sprays should be more prominent on the outside of the rim, so they do not obscure the contents of the basket.

1 Wrap the binding wire around a handful of moss using several turns of the wire to keep it in place. Pull the binding wire so the moss is firm. Take a second handful and bind it in with the first, keeping the garland the same thickness as you work. Continue until all the rim wire is covered. Secure the binding wire by giving it a couple of extra turns, and cut off any surplus.

3 Divide the dried plant material (excluding the lavender) into small same-type sprays of between 5-10 stems (the number per bunch depends on the size of the plants) and wire each bunch onto a stub wire.

4 Taking the first spray, poke the stub wire through the moss to the inside of the basket, then bend the wire back on itself into the moss to secure it. Continue with the other sprays, individually or in clusters, keeping them roughly at the same level and facing in the same direction, until the rim is obscured.

2 Attach the moss-covered wire to the basket using stub wire
every 4in (10cm) or so, pushing the stub ends through the
basket and over the rim. On the rim of the basket, twist the
ends of the wires tightly to secure them, and push the ends
into the moss.

5 The lavender sprays are added last, in informal clusters
pointing in different directions. If there are still any
unwanted gaps, add some smaller sprays of lavender or other
herbs to fill.

Herb-Garlanded Wooden Box

You can also use a wooden box for a variation of the herb-
garlanded basket. Because you cannot poke wires through
the wooden container, as you can with a basket, you will
need to use another method: glue the wired bunches of
herbs to the container with a hot glue gun (see
Techniques, p. 100).

This form of decoration also works well with simpler,
smaller containers, where a moss base might make the
container look top-heavy. You can fill these boxes with
mixtures of herb potpourri (see p. 50).

For this decorative balsa wood box, a mixture of heads
of artichokes (*Cynara cardunculus*), honesty (*Lunaria
annua*), and small bunches of dried lemon grass
(*Cymbopogon citratus*) has been used, but you can use
whatever is available locally or from your garden. Large
seed heads and flowers will not need to be bunched.

*This inexpensive balsa wood box, with
its edge trimmed with herbs, is perfect for displaying
and storing soaps and sponges in a bathroom
or guest bedroom.*

TUSSIE-MUSSIE

A tussie-mussie is ideal for displaying and drying fresh herbs and flowers. The posy can be made from one or two herbs and used for culinary purposes, or it can be purely decorative, containing a selection of herbs and flowers that will last indefinitely.

ECORATIVE POSIES OF aromatic herbs and flowers were originally Elizabethan accessories, carried through the streets to ward off the unpleasant smells and diseases of the times and nicknamed "nosegays," or "tussie-mussies." The beauty of the tussie-mussie is that its herbs and flowers retain their looks and fragrance as they dry. In addition to being highly decorative, these posies are a practical and convenient way to store culinary and medicinal plants because their ingredients can be plucked out of the bouquet whenever they are needed. Preserved by air-drying (see pp. 102-104) and stored out of direct sunlight, they will also last for years.

During the summer, when herbs and flowers are at their most prolific, the selection of fresh ingredients for a tussie-mussie can be varied from week to week. If you choose to make a purely decorative tussie-mussie, with the inclusion of plants other than herbs, make sure that the plants are suitable for air-drying. Whatever the herb or flower, its stems must be robust and healthy, and free from mildew and infestation. You can use any combination of colors. Goldenrod (*Solidago*) with purple oregano (*Origanum vulgare*) and globe thistles (*Echinops*) provide a good contrast of purple-blues and yellows. Pinks (*Dianthus*), edged with roses (*Rosa* sp.) make an all-pink arrangement that dries well and has a wonderful scent. You could also use large bunches of lavender with a few fennel flowers or seed heads in similar colors to create a pretty posy in matching shades of pale purple and blue.

A tussie-mussie will look good wherever you put it, but if the finished posy is to be hung against a wall, consider when making it that it will need to be flat-backed (see Edible Herb Posy pp. 92-93). Wherever you hang it, make sure it is warm, dry, and out of direct sunlight.

HERBS AND FLOWERS USED

About 20 sprigs each of:
fennel flower
marigolds
lady's mantle
lavender
pinks

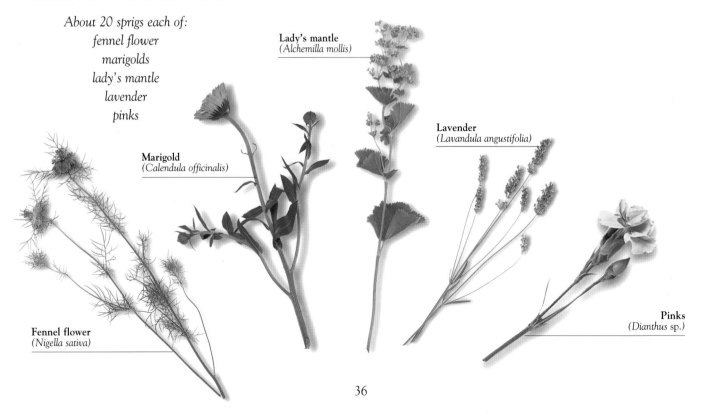

Lady's mantle
(*Alchemilla mollis*)

Marigold
(*Calendula officinalis*)

Lavender
(*Lavandula angustifolia*)

Fennel flower
(*Nigella sativa*)

Pinks
(*Dianthus* sp.)

MAKING THE TUSSIE-MUSSIE

You will need: flat surface on which to sort the herbs and flowers; scissors, for tidying and cutting the stems; twine; one or two strong rubber bands; 30in (75cm) length of ribbon and string, or several strands of raffia, for finishing and hanging up the posy.

When preparing herbs and flowers for the tussie-mussie, strip off the lower leaves carefully to avoid damaging and scarring the stems. Begin only when all the stems are prepared; once the assembly starts, you will need both hands to construct the posy.

When you have arranged the herbs and flowers to your satisfaction and the posy is finished, temporarily tie it with a few turns of string so you can place it on the work surface. Your hands will need a rest by this time. Tie the string fairly tightly, but not so tight that it cuts into the softer stems.

To secure the posy, use a rubber band, doubled if necessary. This will ensure that, when the stems shrink as the herbs dry out, you won't find the floor strewn with herbs and an empty loop of ribbon hanging from the ceiling.

1 Prepare all the stems by carefully removing any untidy lower leaves. Strip any thin leaves directly from each stem, except when preparing multistemmed flowers, such as marigolds, which must be cut into separate stems before stripping.

4 Hold the posy up at intervals to check its shape. Aim to fill in the holes with more herbs or flowers. Add slender stems, such as lavender, in groups of three or more—otherwise they will lack impact and be lost among the larger herbs.

5 Save your most precious herbs and flowers to add at the end. Thread longer stems into the middle, and add shorter ones around the edges to create an even, rounded shape. Secure the tussie-mussie first with string, and then with a rubber band.

2 Group the plants together according to type. Working with one at a time, loosely bunch up a group of herbs in one hand, so they act as a structure for the other stems.

3 With the other hand, gradually build up the shape and size of the posy by adding and arranging stems one at a time, and turning it as you work. If you are hanging the posy against a wall, remember to make it flat on one side. If the posy is to be free-hanging from a beam or hook, then no such restrictions need apply.

6 To finish the posy, take several strands of raffia, lengths of string, or a wide ribbon, and make a tie wide enough to cover the rubber band. Knot securely and then, if you plan to hang your tussie-mussie, you can use the excess length to form a loop.

KITCHEN WALL HANGING

This burlap and terracotta pot wall hanging is an innovative way to storing herbs

in the kitchen. Freshly gathered herbs are left to dry in bunches or

pots, beside garlic bulbs, spices, and flower heads.

OST OF US enjoy having decorative items around us in the kitchen as we work, but as space is often limited, it can be very irritating to prepare supper on work surfaces that are cluttered with pots and plants. However, this decorative hanging eliminates the problem and only makes use of a small area of empty wall space.

I prefer to use old terracotta pots because they have so much character and a straighter, more refined shape than new ones. If you don't have any on hand, try looking in flea markets, at your local nursery, or even at garage sales. Alternatively, modern terracotta pots and ceramic holders work well, especially if you choose colors that coordinate with your kitchen. Another decorative tip is to place one

pot inside another, trapping a little moss between the two. This adds interest and is a good way of using pots that have a broken lip, without spoiling the finished effect.

If you cannot find burlap bags for the top bow and bottom "ribbon" piece, burlap can be bought by the yard (meter) in most fabric stores. Otherwise, substitute a coarse fabric such as natural linen for the burlap.

Hung out of the way, in a dry place and out
of direct light, this swag will give a gentle
fragrance to your kitchen and look good
for several years. The herbs can easily be replaced
with fresh stocks as you use them, or as
the bundles become worn out.

Sunflower
(Helianthus annuus)

Lavender
(Lavandula angustifolia)

Marjoram
(Origanum vulgare)

Thyme
(Thymus vulgaris)

Garlic
(Allium sativum)

Cardoon
(Cynara cardunculus)

HERBS AND FLOWER
HEADS USED
3 bunches of lavender
3 bunches of marjoram
3-4 bunches of thyme
4-5 sunflowers
6-7 cardoons
5-6 garlic bulbs

MAKING THE HANGING

For a swag approximately 40in (110cm) in length, you will need: 1-2in (2.5-5cm) gauge chicken wire, cut to 12 by 36in (30 by 90cm); dried moss or hay; 6-7 small terracotta pots, wired for hanging; approximately 1yd (1m) burlap to form the bow and knotted bottom piece (optional, see p. 107); stub wires; and cotton cord, string, or raffia for tying herb bundles.

Individual herbs are bunched together with decorative twine, such as raffia or cord, to enhance the design. Attach a stub wire to the twine on each bundle so the herb bunches can be attached to the wall hanging.

1 Wire each terracotta pot by inserting a long stub wire through the drainage hole and pulling the two ends together at the top of the pot.

2 Working on a flat surface, place the moss down the center of the chicken wire and fold both sides over to meet. Secure by twisting short wires from one cut edge around the other edge.

4 Wire some herb bundles directly onto the moss base, making sure all the wires are passed through to the back, and bent over into the base. Attach some herbs inside the pots by threading the wire through the bottom of the pot and into the base.

5 Next add the largest flower heads, such as the sunflowers, filling in any gaps. Wire and attach them in the same way as the herb bundles. Then add any remaining smaller items— leaving the garlic until last.

3 Wire the pots securely and at a slight angle to the moss base, using extra stub wires to hold them firm, if necessary. Hold the arrangement upright every so often and stand back to check the position and angle of the pots. Make adjustments if the pots are not hanging well.

6 Finish the hanging with a burlap bow and bottom piece (see p. 107), attaching both items to the swag with stub wires. Fix a hook onto the wall and hang the finished swag from it using the chicken wire on the back of the swag.

Chili Wall Hanging

This is an excellent way to preserve beautiful, shiny red chilies, although the garland should be hung out of children's reach because chilies cause irritation to the eyes, mouth, and skin. Always wear rubber gloves when handling them. Use larger chilies, *Capsicum annuum* Longum Group, rather than the hotter *C. frutescens*, but remember that all chilies become hotter with age.

You will need about 40 fresh, red chillies, 10-12 small bundles of fresh thyme, 10-12 fresh bay leaves, thin wire, and a large-eye needle or bodkin. Cut a 30in (75cm) length of wire, insert one end through the needle, and tie a knot in the other end. Wrap a bay leaf around the first thyme bundle and thread it onto the hanging at the point where the ends of the bay leaf meet, to hold the thyme in place. Next thread on some chilies (pushing the needle through the middle of each) and continue to add bundles of thyme every few inches. Finish with more chilies, leaving about 6in (15cm) of wire. Twist the two wire ends securely to make a loop, and hang by a nail or hook.

Colorful and fun, this chili "necklace" brightens up any kitchen. Here, a fresh bay leaf has been wrapped around each bundle of thyme for an extra decorative touch.

Herbs to Scent Rooms

Without doubt, it is the aromatic quality of herbs that make them not only popular but therapeutic. Scented herbs exude a subtle fragrance that will gently perfume rooms of your house, and they can be used, along with flowers, to make ornaments that last for ages. As well as smelling wonderful, rosemary pomanders, a perfumed pocket cushion, herbal potpourri, and a fresh herb wreath are also delightful decorations.

ROSEMARY POMANDERS

Reminiscent of newly clipped topiary, these are pomanders with a difference.

Easy to make from a variety of fresh herbs, their neat, round

shapes leave a lasting impression.

*T*HERE IS SOMETHING intensely satisfying about observing newly clipped topiary hedges, especially those generously rounded shapes seen in formal gardens. Although traditional pomanders, made from clove-studded fruit (see pp. 68-9), have a charm of their own, these versions have their own particular beauty and even just one on its own looks striking. Fortunately, these herb pomanders, with their topiary ball shapes and distinctive scents, are extremely easy to make. All you need is a little patience and a plentiful supply of fresh herbs, which makes this an ideal project if you grow herbs yourself, as you can use whichever ones are at their best at the time.

Herbs such as oregano and curry plant look very effective, especially when used together, because their unopened flower buds provide a marvelous range of textures. One fact to keep in mind when making your first pomander is that even a relatively small sphere does have a deceptively large surface area, which requires a surprisingly large number of herbs. It is much better to experiment with a small sphere until you get an idea of just how much material you will need for each pomander.

If you are making a collection of spheres with a selection of herbs, incorporate some spices, too. Star anise and peppercorns, especially the pink and green types, look really stunning when glued all over the surface of the sphere. These pomanders make a wonderful display if you arrange them in a circular bowl with other spheres or rounded objects, such as sea-washed pebbles from the beach. Alternatively, you could place them in a large, shallow dish on a bed of potpourri (see p. 50), or even on loose herbs and spices.

HERBS USED

Approximately 30 sprigs of rosemary
for each pomander

Rosemary
(Rosmarinus officinalis)

MAKING THE POMANDER

For each pomander, you will need: a 4in (10cm) diameter sphere of dried florist's foam and heavy-duty florist's scissors.

Remove any old or brown growth from the rosemary. Work a line of sprigs around the circumference (along the middle), dividing the sphere into two. Then work the other way to divide it in quarters. This makes it easier to fill in the sections and trim the rosemary without losing the shape of the globe.

Other herbs with fairly woody stems, such as oregano or fully mature thyme can also be used for this project.

1 Using fairly short sprigs of rosemary, push each sprig firmly into the foam. Form a line that divides the sphere in half first, then create another line to divide it into quarters. Try to space the rosemary as evenly as possible.

Place the herb pomanders where you can enjoy their attractive shapes and aromas—place two together on a side table as here, or make them with ribbons to hang. Although they become more brittle as they dry out, the herb pomanders look good for several years. One of my favorite ways to display them is among a group of clove pomanders (see p. 68).

2 Gently clip the sprigs to a uniform height as you work, but be careful—it is easy to chop too much away and find a flat area has developed on one side. Quartering the sphere helps avoid this problem.

3 Continue filling in each quarter until you have completely covered the sphere. Now you can "fine tune" the clipping by examining it from all sides. Carefully snip away until you are satisfied with the finished shape.

WRAPPED CANDLES

Bound around simple, plain candles, fresh herbs look stunning when illuminated by soft, flickering light. The warmth given off by a burning flame also helps to release the essential oils of the fragrant herbs—providing a real feast for the senses.

*D*INING BY CANDLELIGHT is always magical, and even more so when the candles themselves look and smell as good as these. Although I have used thyme here, you could experiment with a range of herbs including lavender, rosemary, fresh bay leaves, sage, or oregano. In fact, you could use a mixture of these fragrances, either selecting a different herb for each candle, or combining several around one single candle.

I have used fairly squat, thick candles, which are stable and stand upright without a candlestick, but to add height and variety, you could use taller and more slender candles, each secured in a candlestick and then bound with herbs around both candle and holder. This keeps the dripping wax away from the herbs, so you can still use them in cooking later on.

Caution: Never leave the candles unattended, and keep a close eye on the flame to ensure that it does not come too near the herbs, or you may generate more warmth at the dinner table than you bargained for!

MAKING THE WRAPPED CANDLE

To make the free-standing herb candle illustrated here, you will need: thick candle, at least 3in (7.5cm) in diameter and 4in (10cm) tall; raffia, jute string, twine, or cord to bind the herbs onto the candle; and sharp scissors.

It is important that you leave a 2in (5cm) loose end of twine when you first tie around the bottom of the candle—after the candle is covered, use this loose end to secure the herbs. Do not try to cover a too large a section of the candle with herbs in one attempt. Keep adding a few small sprigs at a time, binding them around tightly with the twine as you work. When the entire candle has been surrounded with herbs, make another couple of turns with the twine, pulling very tightly. Finish with a double knot or a bow. Because this candle is designed to stand on its own, thyme is a good choice of herb—its stems are robust and woody and provide the candle with extra support.

HERBS USED
*For each candle:
approximately 30 sprigs of
fresh thyme*

Thyme
(Thymus vulgaris)

1 Tie an end of the twine around the bottom half of the candle in a secure knot. Do not cut the twine.

2 Holding the candle in your palm, with the wick pointing away, place herbs along the candle and pull twine over them.

48

3 Add more herbs in the same way, leaves pointing toward the wick and stems toward the base, working around the candle and binding with the twine as you add sprigs of thyme. Make sure that you keep the twine relatively tight to prevent the herbs from slipping out.

4 Finish off with a couple of extra turns of the twine, pull tight, and pull through the loose end of twine. Tie the two ends in a knot or bow. Trim the ends of the herb stems at the base of the candle with scissors so they are flush with the candle base. This will enable the finished herb candle to stand straight without needing any other support.

As well as looking fresh and welcoming, this thyme-wrapped candle gives off a wonderful scent as it burns. It would also make a good dinner table decoration, and rather an appropriate one if thyme is a key ingredient on the menu!

49

HERBAL POTPOURRI

Shades of silver-gray, blue, and green are set off by flecks of deep red in this simple but striking potpourri. The mixture is easily rejuvenated with a few drops of essential oil when its subtle perfume starts to fade.

DRIED, BLENDED, and then scattered in a bowl or basket, herbs, flowers, and spices have been used since biblical times to perfume rooms and clothes. Unfortunately, these days we have become accustomed to commercially available potpourris. These are full of strong, artificial fragrances, which can make the scents of home-made potpourris seem bland by comparison. Nevertheless, making potpourris yourself is very rewarding, and I certainly prefer their softer, mellower perfumes.

Potpourri, literally translated into English, is "rotted pot," which is obviously why we still prefer to use the French word! A true potpourri should be moist. To achieve this, layers of semidried petals are mixed with salt and left to ferment for several days until they form a crumbly "cake." This is mixed with different herbs, flower petals, and spices to form a potpourri, which is then cured for several weeks. Needless to say, these moist potpourris are rather unattractive, which is why dry potpourris are more popular, even though they are less concentrated and do not last as long.

HERBS USED
20 sprigs of dried lavender
20 sprigs of dried oregano
1oz (30g) of dried pinks petals
6 sprigs of dried honesty
6 sprigs of dried eucalyptus

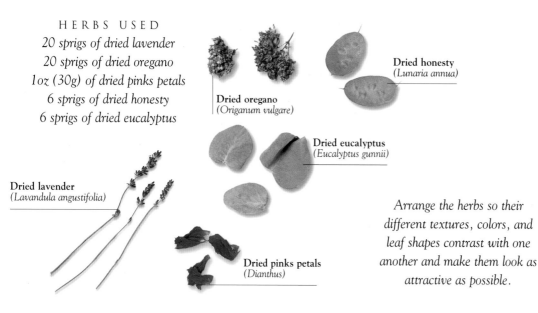

Dried honesty
(*Lunaria annua*)

Dried oregano
(*Origanum vulgare*)

Dried eucalyptus
(*Eucalyptus gunnii*)

Dried lavender
(*Lavandula angustifolia*)

Dried pinks petals
(*Dianthus*)

Arrange the herbs so their different textures, colors, and leaf shapes contrast with one another and make them look as attractive as possible.

MAKING HERBAL POTPOURRI

In addition to the herbs, you will need: glass or ceramic bowl; scissors; essential oil (I use orange essence); rubber band or tape; and a paper bag to cure the herbs.

Roses are often the main ingredients in potpourris, because they tend to retain more of their natural perfume than other flowers, despite the fact that many cut roses are grown for their size and visual appeal, to the detriment of their scent.

Dry potpourris are much easier to make than moist ones, because they only rely on a quantity of herbs and flowers, dried until crisp, and then mixed with spices to enhance the fragrance. This allows you to experiment with all kinds of combinations of herbs, flowers, and spices. When your mixture is ready, transfer it to a paper bag and seal it. Leave it for a few days to allow the fragrances of the herbs, flowers, and essential oils to develop and intermingle, or cure, before use.

1 Strip the dried leaves from the eucalyptus and put them in a suitable bowl. By doing this, you will be helping to release the leaves' essential oils. If you wish, you can also crumble a few leaves to encourage the process.

3 Strip the flat, coin-like, green leaves from the honesty and add them to the eucalyptus—the smooth, silvery eucalyptus contrasts well with the pale green, pod-filled leaves of the honesty. Then use a pair of sharp scissors to snip the lavender stalks into short pieces and add them to the bowl.

4 Mix the ingredients thoroughly and add a handful of dried pinks petals. As well as contributing fragrance they also enhance the appearance of the potpourri mixture with their dark red hue. You may add in any other colorful petals or leaves at this stage.

2 Holding the bunch of lavender over the bowl, use your hands to rub off the flower heads, allowing them to fall in among the eucalyptus leaves.

5 Add a few drops of essential oil (orange essence is used here to add a citrus tang to the herbs) and toss the mixture well to ensure the oil blends with the herbs. Cure the mixture for a few days before displaying it in a pretty bowl or pot.

Floral Herb Potpourri

For a softer, much more flowery potpourri, dry a few sprigs of herbs and some flower heads picked each day from the garden in the summer months.

By early fall you will have a wonderful selection of interesting and colorful ingredients to use in creating several bowls of potpourri, filled with the marvelous reminders of summer.

The addition of some store-bought dried rose buds, dried herbs of your choice, and a few drops of essential oil will increase the aroma of this bold, bright combination. Here I have used a mixture of pinks, peonies, and roses, with marigold petals, heads of blue iris flowers, and lemon verbena leaves for a fresh, citrus fragrance.

A simple, shallow glass dish is used to display an evocative and fragrant reminder of heady summer days. In addition to the lemon verbena, sprinkle on a few drops of rose essential oil to enhance the warm, floral bouquet.

HERB POCKET PILLOW

This fragrant pillow, perfect for your favorite chair, sofa, or bed, features a small,

herb-filled sachet, which fits into a pocket stitched onto the

front of a regular-sized scatter pillow.

IF, LIKE ME, YOU ARE less than accomplished in the needlework department, do not worry. This project does not require any special skills, as you can buy a pillow cover—ideally a fairly plain one—to use as the base of this design, and then choose extra matching or coordinating fabric to make the pocket for the herb sachet. There are all sorts of wonderful flower- or herb-printed fabrics available from department stores, which are appropriate for this project. It is always worth looking for a remnant, too, because you only need a small amount of material.

If you are having pillow covers professionally made to match your upholstery, ask for the pockets to be added so you only have to make the sachets.

The blend of herbs I am using is just one possibility. It has a very fruity fragrance with a hint of the East, which comes from the cardamom pods. You could also try a dried rosemary and thyme variation, using 2oz (55g) of each and a little dried lemon verbena.

MAKING THE POCKET PILLOW

For the pocket on the standard square pillow cover, you will need a rectangle of fabric measuring 9in by 12in (23cm by 30cm). For the herb sachet, you will need a rectangle of plain muslin, measuring 6in by 12in (15cm by 30cm). In addition to the herbs, you will also need: scissors; needle; and thread.

To make the pocket on the pillow, work with the right side of the fabric facing down. Fold in the two long sides and one short side by 1in (2.5cm) and pin. Fold the remaining top short side under by 1in (2.5cm) and machine-stitch this edge only (approximately ½in (1cm) from the edge). On the wrong side, carefully press all edges, removing the pins as you work. Position the pocket on the front of the pillow cover and pin in place. The top short side will form the opening to the pocket. Hand-stitch the pocket onto the pillow, along the two long sides and the bottom, being careful to stitch through only one thickness of the cover.

HERBS AND SPICES USED
2oz (55g) cardamom pods
2oz (55g) dried rosemary
2oz (55g) dried lemon grass

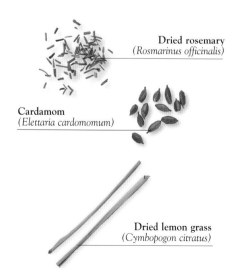

Dried rosemary
(Rosmarinus officinalis)

Cardamom
(Elettaria cardomomum)

Dried lemon grass
(Cymbopogon citratus)

1 To make the sachet, mix the herbs together and place in a pile at one end of a rectangular piece of muslin.

2 Fold the muslin over the herb mixture to form a square, pin securely along the three open sides, and stitch.

3 On a flat surface, place the prepared pocket on the middle of the front of the pillow cover. Pin and hand-stitch the pocket onto the pillow (see Making the Pocket Pillow, opposite). Do not stitch through more than one layer of the cover, or it will be impossible to put back the pillow form.

4 Push the finished herbal sachet down into the pocket on the front of the pillow cover, making sure that it lies flat. The beauty of having this secure but open pocket is that you can replace the herb sachet with a new one whenever you like. You can try out a variety of fragrances, concocted from different mixes of dried herbs to see which one you like best or which seems to suit the atmosphere of a room.

The choice of fabric used for this herb-scented pillow, with its little potted orange tree, is very much in keeping with its herbal theme. The pillow looks good on this antique cane-sided chair and smells delicious, too.

55

FLOWERY HERB WREATH

*Created from a less traditional selection of herbs and dotted with roses,
this pretty wreath provides a touch of summery freshness. Fragrant and
decorative, it will last for several days.*

THIS COLORFUL wreath of fresh herbs would look wonderful hung on the front door to welcome guests to a summer party or wedding, or even as a flat table decoration, perhaps with some herb-wrapped candles (see pp. 48-49) in the center.

The decoration is created on a wire frame covered with fresh, damp sphagnum moss. Because the wired bunches of herbs are able to draw up moisture from the moss, they will last and look good for several days. Wire frames are available in a variety of shapes and sizes from good florists and arts and crafts stores. When deciding which one to buy, keep in mind that the moss and herbs will add at least 5in (12cm) to the overall size.

I have used a selection of different herbs; you will be able to achieve interesting effects by experimenting with different combinations. You could even stick to a single variety—using either rue on its own, or bay leaves, gives a dramatic, sculptural effect. The same principles apply if you make this ring with dried herbs, although in this case, the moss base will need to be completely dry, to prevent any mildew or mold buildup. For a final decorative touch, add a ribbon bow to the top of the ring.

Safflowers and fragrant herbs are woven into a traditional and very natural decorative ring, with texture and leaf form as important to the overall design as the color and variety of herbs used.

HERBS USED

Large handfuls (at least 20 sprigs of each herb) of: feverfew, rosebuds, gay feathers, curry plant, mint, lavender foliage, bay, safflower, sea holly, roses, parsley

Curry plant
(Helichrysum italicum)

Mint
(Mentha spicata)

Lavender foliage
(Lavandula angustifolia 'Hidcote')

Bay
(Laurus nobilis)

Gay feathers
(Liatris spicata)

Safflower
(Carthamus tinctorius)

Feverfew
(Tanacetum parthenium)

Sea holly
(Eryngium martimum)

Rosebuds
(Rosa gallica)

Roses
(Rosa gallica)

Parsley
(Petroselinum crispum)

MAKING THE HERB RING

In addition to your selection of herbs, you will need: a wire wreath base about 10in (25cm) in diameter; large bag of sphagnum moss; a good supply of florist's wire (in a mixture of gauges to wire different thicknesses of stem); reel wire to bind on the moss; and a pair of sharp scissors. It is best to prepare the herbs a few varieties at a time, making them up into small bunches and wiring them with florist's stub wires (see Techniques, page 101). Here I have used medium-gauge florist's wire for most of the bunches and stems.

1 Make the base by attaching damp sphagnum moss to the wire frame using reel wire. Take small handfuls of moss, hold them against the frame, and secure by binding around with the wire. Cover the whole frame.

2 Work with your green herbs first, wiring the individual herbs together into small, even bunches. Use 4-5 stems of mint, 7-8 stems of parsley, and clusters of 3-4 bay leaves. Make approximately 10 bunches of each herb.

4 Fill in between the wired herb bunches with silvery-green curry plant and lavender foliage. These will provide a variety of leaf form and color for extra interest.

5 Begin to add the more robust flowering herbs (safflower, sea holly, and gay feathers). Continue to space out and insert the bunches at different angles to fill the ring out evenly.

3 Taking one type of herb at a time, insert the wired bunches into the moss base. Push the wire right through the base, making sure the ends of the herb stems touch the damp moss, and bend the wire back into the base to secure. Space the bunches evenly around the ring and try to insert the bunches at different angles to create a rounded effect.

Dried herb wreath with hops & lavender

This simple dried herb wreath can be made from a couple of herbs, but one of them must have a twining or lax habit. This wreath is made from a vine base, covered with hops and lavender. If you have no vine, you could use stems of willow or other flexible and relatively pliable branches that will allow you to shape them into a roughly circular design. Hold the circular shape together with heavy-gauge florist's wire. The lavender will need to be put into bunches first, wired with medium-gauge florist's wire (trim the stems, if necessary), and attached to the base at evenly spaced intervals. Loop the hops to the wreath, allowing small pieces to trail attractively to make it less formal in appearance. The hops can be pinned in position with wire hooks. Finally, make a hanging device with a loop of florist's wire attached through the back of the ring.

6 Add the delicate flowering herbs last: bunches of feverfew and rosebuds are attached to the ring, followed by the large cream rose heads, each wired individually.

Hops and lavender make an excellent color and textural combination. The stiff form of the lavender is balanced by the twining habit of the hops.

Herbs to Scent Linen

There is nothing quite like the crisp feel of newly washed and pressed linen, and when combined with a fresh, clean scent, it is doubly enticing. There are various ways to keep your sheets, pillowcases, tablecloths, and household linens smelling sweet. This chapter shows you how to make clove pomanders, lavender bundles, and herb- and spice-filled bags—tuck these into drawers or hang them in cupboards to gently perfume your linen.

LAVENDER BAGS

Although possibly the simplest of items to make, lavender bags are still my all-time favorites.
They remind me of childhood summers spent collecting and drying lavender from my
grandmother's garden, and then using it to make these sweet-smelling bags.

*I*N MEDIEVAL TIMES lavender was often used as a condiment to flavor food; these days, however, it is rarely used in recipes (although I must admit to having eaten and enjoyed lavender ice cream on more than one occasion). The principal use of the herb is now in perfumes, and its distinctive aroma is well-known for its calming and restorative properties. Lavender harvesters of old are said to have worn a bunch of the flowers tucked into the inside band of their hats to keep headaches at bay. With its rich perfume, lavender is *the* herb to use for scenting linen. Various species of lavender are grown, but my personal favorite is *Lavandula angustifolia* 'Hidcote.' This species bears rich violet-blue flowers which, like the rest of the plant, are highly scented. No part of this plant needs to be wasted because both its flowers and stems can be used when making up lavender sachets.

This pale blue gingham check, with matching silk
ribbon, looks fresh and simple—a good color choice to
use with lavender. I like to keep some lavender bags among
handkerchiefs and linen, but they can also be placed in the
drawers of a desk to gently scent writing paper.

MAKING THE LAVENDER BAGS

You will need: a piece of fabric for each bag (I have used some cotton gingham) measuring 6in by 9in (15cm by 23cm), including a ½in (12mm) seam allowance; needle, thread, and scissors; 5ft (1.5m) narrow silk ribbon, to match or complement your fabric; a ceramic or glass bowl; a spoon or wide-necked funnel, for filling the bag; and a handful of oatmeal to fill out the bags.

1 Fold the fabric lengthwise, with right sides together, and secure with pins. Stitch one long and one short side, leaving the top open. Fold over 1½in (3cm) of fabric, pin, and press. Remove pins and turn right sides out.

2 Using a pair of sharp scissors, snip the bundles of lavender flowers and stems into very short lengths, directly into the bowl. Add the oatmeal to the lavender and mix thoroughly. Fill the fabric bags and secure the neck of each with a rubber band. Add a silk ribbon for decoration.

HERBS USED
To fill between four and six bags:
3oz (85g) dried lavender

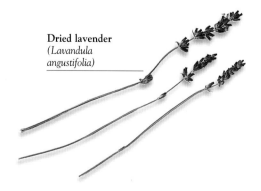

Dried lavender
(*Lavandula*
angustifolia)

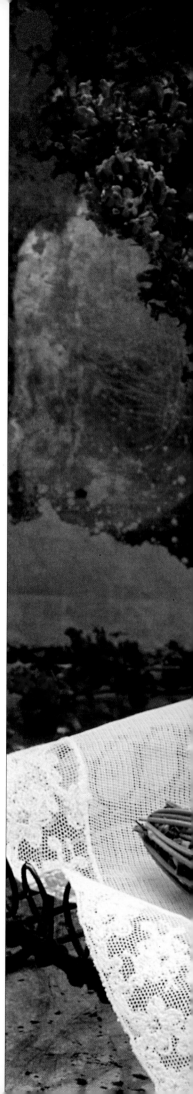

LAVENDER BUNDLES

These charming little bundles of lavender take only seconds to make and yet they look beautiful for years. The scent of lavender reminds us of the warm summer days when it was harvested.

THESE LAVENDER BUNDLES—a more decorative version of lavender bags—are unique because they can only be made using fresh newly harvested lavender, as the stems must be full of sap so they are supple enough to be bent in half without breaking. As a small child, harvesting the lavender from my grandmother's garden was one of the rituals of summer. While picking it one day, a neighbor asked me what I was going to use the lavender for. Having explained that I would dry it and use it to fill lavender bags, the neighbor offered me an easier and more beautiful way of using this herb. Her idea was to use the lavender fresh, bending over the stems to enclose the flower heads within a bundle or "bottle." She would then weave silk or satin ribbons between the stems to trap the flower heads so they did not leak. When dry, the bundles could be slipped into drawers or linen cupboards where they would release their summery perfume.

The only alteration I have made to the neighbor's method is to omit the silk or satin ribbons. Although her method may be more practical longterm, I felt that it diminished the natural beauty of these bundles. It also made the bundles much more time-consuming to produce.

HERBS USED
12-18 stems of freshly
picked lavender for
each bundle

Lavender
(*Lavandula angustifolia*)

These lavender bundles are so attractive that it seems a shame to hide them away in drawers or cupboards. You can display a few in a basket, on top of napkins, or laid out on a cloth on a rack. Not only will they look good, they will also also scent the linen at the same time.

MAKING THE LAVENDER BUNDLES

In addition to the lavender, you will need some string or twine. Your own supply of fresh lavender is essential when making these because they need to be produced using the freshest materials. However, even the smallest of plants will yield enough for you to produce at least a couple of bundles each summer.

It is a good idea to cut the lavender as soon as the morning dew has had a chance to dry, and then lay it in a shallow basket before using it. At this time of day, the lavender will be at its most supple and moist—later in the day it will have lost much of its water content, particularly in hot, dry weather.

If you wish to make your bundles a little more glamorous, you could use a piece of delicate lace or a ribbon to secure the stems, instead of the rustic-looking natural string I have used. Alternatively, you can tie a few lavender bundles together and hang them on a wall.

1 Sort through the lavender stems and assemble between 12 and 18 stems within your hand, making sure that the bases of the flower heads are aligned.

3 Taking one stem at a time, gently bend it back over the flower heads and hold it on top of the flower bundle with your thumb. Repeat with each stem.

4 After you have bent all the stems over the bundle of lavender flowers, make sure that they are all equally spaced and that they completely enclose the flower heads.

2 Use a piece of string or twine to tie the lavender together securely at the base of their flower heads. It is essential that the stems are held together tightly because these will form the top of the bundle once completed.

5 Hold the stems in place and use another piece of string to tie them securely and tightly beneath the flower heads. Trim the stem ends to look neat and uniform, then place them on a rack somewhere warm to dry.

Lemon Grass & Rosemary Bundles

The season for harvesting lavender is short, so if you miss out on making the bundles one year, a similar technique can be used to make a rosemary and lemon grass bundle. This reminds me of the delicious Catalan herb bunches used to flavor soups and stews in that region.

All you need is a large stem of fresh lemon grass and some fresh or dried rosemary. Cut the lemon grass in half lengthwise and place a small sprig or two of fresh rosemary in between. Tie the two halves of lemon grass together with twine, thread, or even colored embroidery thread, and place the bundle on a rack in a warm place to dry out.

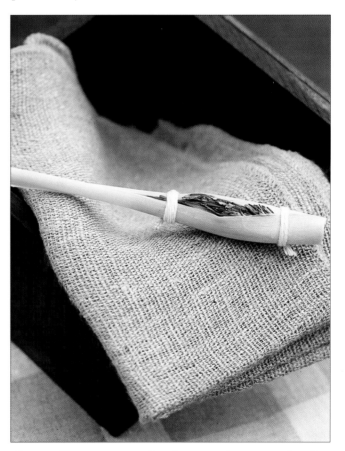

Giving off a more a masculine fragrance, lemon grass bundles can be kept in a drawer among handkerchiefs or scarves. They would also make the perfect finishing touch to such items when they are given as gifts.

CLOVE POMANDERS

I am a huge fan of traditional clove pomanders because they are such simple objects to make, yet have so much appeal. With their evocative spicy aroma and their attractive shape and texture, these clove-studded oranges will add color and fragrance anywhere in the home.

An Elizabethan classic, pomanders are among my favorite decorative objects. They are entirely made from natural ingredients, which can all be found around the home. Traditionally created using oranges, I find that lemons, mandarins, apples, pears, and even bananas work just as well, and when dry, look beautiful massed together in one bowl. Pomanders also make lovely gifts and, with their citrus and clove smell so redolent of mulled wine, they are particularly popular at Christmas.

I have made pomanders for years and have never needed to use a curing mixture to aid the drying of the fruits as most old recipes suggest. The fruits dry just as firmly and quickly on their own, and to my mind have a more authentic aroma of the fruit and cloves alone, rather than a fragrance confused by other spices.

Some fruit can be a little hard to push the cloves into, and some can even be a little sticky. Only sound fruit should be used, and with pears or apples, the harder and less

ripe they are the better. Lemons and large oranges are the most difficult to make because their peel is so thick. Satsumas and mandarins are ideal, since they are comparatively soft and small enough to finish quickly! It is essential that each fruit is completed within 12 hours, because fruit softens as a result of being pierced with the cloves, and may become too soft to handle and split.

Some people use masking tape to mark out an area that will remain clove free, to be decorated with a pretty satin or hanging ribbon. I find this effect a little too ornate and prefer to use a simple cord or wire woven between the cloves to hang the finished pomander.

Pomanders were once placed among clean linens in order to keep the moths and other insects away and to mask the rather musty smells resulting from storage in unventilated and unheated homes. They are still used as a moth deterrent, but these days pomanders are mostly displayed decoratively and used to scent rooms.

MAKING THE POMANDERS

In addition to the cloves, you will need a fruit of your choice. Here I have used five satsumas. Begin by using lines of cloves to divide the fruit into quarters. Leave a ¼in (½cm) gap between each clove, otherwise you may find that the skin splits. You can then form the cloves into some sort of a pattern or work randomly. Remember that as the fruit dries, it will shrink, and the cloves will become much closer and more compact. To dry the pomander, choose a place where you will be able to keep an eye on the pomander, such as a shelf near a radiator. The pomander needs turning daily to ensure that it dries out evenly. Initially it may appear to become very soft, but this is usual. If you have more than one pomander in a paper bag, keep them apart to allow air to circulate between them. After a week or two, the pomander will be ready for use.

SPICE USED
4oz (12g) of cloves for each small pomander

Cloves
(*Syzygium aromaticum*)

1 It is essential that only perfectly sound, smooth fruit is used. Select whole cloves with long spikes before you start. As you insert the cloves, remember to leave a ¼in (½cm) gap between each one.

2 Divide the fruit into quarters with lines of cloves. Push each clove through the skin of the fruit so its stem is completely embedded. If the skin is hard to pierce, use a needle to make the holes.

3 When the fruit is covered with cloves, put it into a brown paper bag and leave it somewhere warm and dark to dry. It will need to be turned daily in order to dry out evenly.

Pomanders placed with your table linen will impart a warm and spicy fragrance, and will help keep insects away.

69

MOTH BAGS

Many scented herbs and spices are excellent at detering moths and other pests because the insects are repelled by the plants' essential oils. These little bags in a closet or cupboard will keep moths away. They will also keep your clothes smelling fresh.

MEDIEVAL HOUSEWIVES grew certain herbs in their gardens specifically for the purpose of protecting their clothing from the ravages of moths. Indeed, the French name for southernwood is *garde-robe* which, literally translated, means "protecting clothes."

Although primarily designed to keep moths and other pests away from clothing and linen, these little herb bags also emit a delightful perfume. The highly aromatic herbs of rosemary, southernwood, thyme, and mint work well when combined with the pungent clove and cinnamon spices. Because these bags are more practical than decorative (and will mostly be hidden in the closet), use simple, inexpensive fabric. Loosely woven cotton ticking or natural linen are both ideal because they allow air to circulate within the bag and the scent of its contents to penetrate the fabric. The neck of the bag can be tied with a plain cord or a dark-colored, narrow, silk ribbon.

Hang the bags from a clothes hanger, and give them an occasional squeeze to release their fragrance. If you replace the contents of the bags with a fresh mixture once a year, the bags will not lose their potency or effectiveness.

MAKING THE MOTH BAGS

You will need: a piece of fabric for each bag; needle; thread; scissors; and a narrow silk ribbon to decorate each of the bags.

For each bag, I used a piece of cotton ticking, measuring approximately 10in by 9in (25cm by 22cm), which includes a ½in (12mm) seam allowance.

HERBS AND SPICES USED
To fill between 4 and 6 bags:
2oz (55g) dried rosemary
2oz (55g) dried southernwood
2oz (55g) dried thyme
2oz (55g) dried mint
½oz (15g) whole cloves
2 cinnamon sticks, crumbled

1 Fold each piece of fabric in half lengthwise, with right sides together. Pin, then stitch along the long open side and one short side (see above left). Turn the bag right sides out, and use the blunt end of a pencil to push out the corners, creating a neat, square-cornered bag (see above right). Trim the open end with pinking shears, or hem it neatly (above right). Press with an iron.

2 Mix the herbs and spices well in a bowl, rubbing them together with your hands to crumble them. Fill the bag with the mixture, then tie the top securely with the ribbon, adding a loop if you plan to hang the bags.

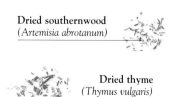

Dried southernwood
(*Artemisia abrotanum*)

Dried mint
(*Mentha spicata*)

Cloves
(*Syzygium aromaticum*)

Dried rosemary
(*Rosmarinus officinalis*)

Dried thyme
(*Thymus vulgaris*)

Cinnamon sticks
(*Cinnamomum verum*)

GENTS' SLEEVE SACHETS

*Scents specifically designed to appeal to men are becoming more popular,
and with these subtle and masculine herbs in mind, I have created a blend of herbs that
removes the staleness from clothing and adds a fresh fragrance.*

THESE SACHETS make a perfect present along with a shirt or tie, or perhaps you could make two sachets and add a new pair of cufflinks that you can fasten on the sachets' cuffs. You can cut off sleeves from old shirts found in secondhand clothing stores or thrift stores—just look for cotton shirts that have undamaged sleeves. Otherwise, search through your family's wornout clothing for suitable sleeves.

The herb mixture below can be used to fill any appropriate bags or sachets to hang in the closet or place in drawers among socks or underwear. You can try creating your own fragranced blend of herbs or use a mixture based on sage and hops, with rosemary and thyme adding sharper accents to the softer, warmer scent of the slightly soporific hops. A more invigorating blend can be made from crumbled mint leaves with star anise, oregano, and lemon grass. To add bulk to the mixture add either the shredded stems of the mint and oregano, or a small quantity of oatmeal. I once made some sachets containing only crumbled bay leaves and dried lemon peel. They were extremely astringent and clean in scent, and yet had a remarkable subtlety, which meant that they didn't overpower the clothes among which they were hung.

If you have no man in your life for whom you wish to create these sachets, you could devise an alternative ladies' sachet using a floral printed blouse, or perhaps a lace hankerchief. Although the mixture suggested would appeal to anyone who likes a fresh, tangy perfume, a more sweetly scented herb version could be created with scented geranium leaves and flowers, rose petals, lavender heads, and lemon balm leaves.

*These masculine and robust-looking striped
sleeve sachets don't have to be tucked away in a
drawer. They could easily be displayed in a
dressing room or hung up among shirts and
ties in the closet, where they will
exude their pleasant fragrance.*

HERBS AND SPICES USED
*For approximately 4 sleeve sachets, mix
together in a ceramic or glass bowl:*
1oz (30g) dried thyme
1oz (30g) dried lemon balm
1oz (30g) dried lavender flowers
1oz (30g) mace
4 dried bay leaves, crumbled

Dried thyme
(*Thymus vulgaris*)

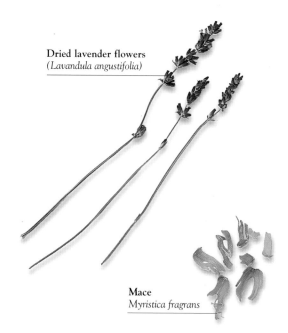

Dried lavender flowers
(*Lavandula angustifolia*)

Dried bay leaves
(*Laurus nobilis*)

Dried lemon balm
(*Melissa officinalis*)

Mace
Myristica fragrans

MAKING THE GENTS' SLEEVE SACHETS

In addition to the herbs and spices, you will need: shirt sleeves (which have cuffs); scissors; needle; and thread. You could use any old cotton shirts with worn-out collars, keeping the rest of the shirt as a painting smock for a child or yourself.

When filling with the herbs, keep the sachets uniform and smooth by crumbling or chopping the ingredients as finely as possible before you insert them—otherwise the larger pieces will stick out through the sleeve material. You could also use a mortar and pestle, or a rolling pin, to grind and crush the lumpy herbs and spices. If you need to bulk out the filling mixture to give the sleeve a better shape, add some oatmeal.

If the shirt sleeve has no button, add a cufflink to the completed sachet as a finishing touch. You could even decorate this sachet by pushing a sprig of fresh herb through the buttonhole.

1 About 15in (45cm) from the bottom edge of the cuff (with the button done up), cut off the undamaged sleeve. Stitch across the cut edges to make a "pocket" for the herbs.

3 Stitch across the sleeve just above the sleeve side opening to enclose the herb mixture.

4 Turn the sleeve right side out. This will make the sleeve appear much shorter.

2 Unbutton, turn right sides to the inside, and fill the cuff with the herb mixture to within 1in (2.5cm) of the sleeve's open side seam, being careful not to overstuff it.

5 Lightly press the seams and button the cuff (or add a cufflink to an appropriately constructed shirt).

Sock Sachets

As a humorous gift for a male friend (since socks are not usually associated with the most attractive of fragrances), you can buy a pair of brand new socks and use them as sachets to be filled with a favorite blend of herbs. Here, I have used a blend of lemon grass and thyme, along with rosemary and cloves.

Buy small-sized socks, draw the shape of the sock onto a piece of cardboard, cut it out, and slip one into each sock, without stretching or distorting it. You will find that the cardboard holds the sock shape, so when you add the herbs, the sachet won't be lumpy. Use a sheet of paper rolled into a cone as a funnel to fill the sock with your blend of herbs, leaving the cardboard in place. Do not overstuff, because this will spoil the shape of the sock sachet.

A natural cotton sock, filled with herbs, has been tied at the ankle with a cord. You can add a bay leaf, as here, or a small sprig of another fresh herb to the tie before giving it to the man (or woman) in your life, or yourself. The sachets will keep clothes smelling fresh for months to come.

HERB-FILLED PILLOW

This delicate pillow is as decorative as it is fragrant, filled with colorful dried herbs and petals, which
are clearly visible through its transparent fabric. Such pillows have
long been used to induce sleep and relaxation.

N MEDIEVAL TIMES, scented herbs and grasses were dried and mixed with hay or straw for stuffing mattresses, known as palliasses, in an attempt to keep them sweet-smelling. *Galium verum,* or lady's bedstraw, was one herb commonly used for this purpose. During the fourteenth century, King Charles VI of France had a pillow filled with goosedown and lavender on his favorite chair, while some 400 years later, George III of England is reputed to have been unable to sleep without his hop-filled pillow.

Organza, lightweight cotton (such as a pair of antique handkerchiefs), or organdy are ideal materials for these delicate items. Because this pillow is semitransparent, it is important to use ingredients that are colorful and attractive as well as fragrant.

MAKING THE HERB-FILLED PILLOW

You will need: a piece of lightweight fabric, such as organza or cotton, measuring 24in by 32in (60cm by 85cm); a needle; thread; and a spoon to fill the pillow with the herb mixture.

Carefully mix all the ingredients together, with the exception of the bay leaves, which are added separately. You can vary the ingredients to include whatever you like, but the filling must contain some robust leaves and petals, such as bay and rose. When you stitch the inner pocket of the pillow, remember to leave an opening corresponding to the one on the outer edge so you can fill the pocket. As a soothing alternative to the herbs used below, try a mixture of herbs such as lavender, bergamot, chamomile, and geranium, which are well-known for their calming properties.

HERBS AND FLOWER
HEADS USED
To fill one pillow:
2 tablespoons each of red,
pink, and yellow rose petals
6 rose stalks
6 dried rose heads
10 bay leaves

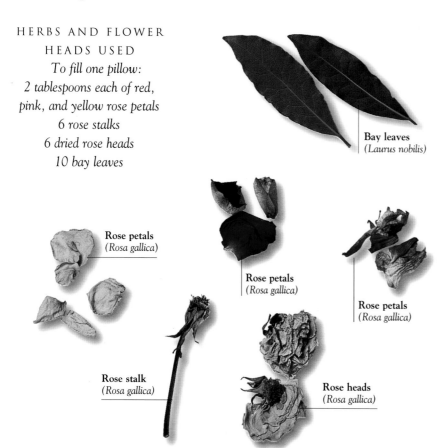

Bay leaves
(*Laurus nobilis*)

Rose petals
(*Rosa gallica*)

Rose petals
(*Rosa gallica*)

Rose petals
(*Rosa gallica*)

Rose stalk
(*Rosa gallica*)

Rose heads
(*Rosa gallica*)

1 Cut your piece of fabric in half and pin right sides together. Zigzag stitch along the edges of two short sides and one long side. Then stitch just two-thirds of the remaining long side, leaving a gap through which you can add the herbs.

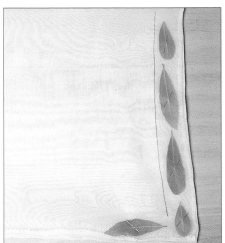

This delicate pillow can be placed on a guest bed to scent the linen and add a hospitable touch. The strong colors of the flower heads and petals look more subtle when seen through the sheer organza fabric.

2 Turn the pillow right sides out. Insert and pin bay leaves all around the edge of the pillow. Straight stitch around the center of the pillow to form an inner "pocket," remembering to leave an opening corresponding to the first one. Secure each bay leaf with a couple of stitches.

3 Add the dried herbs, petals, and leaves until the inner pocket is full, making sure none are trapped in the outer "frame" of bay leaves. Finally, pin and close the two openings and stitch by hand, using large stitches. This will allow easy access to replace or refresh the contents.

Herbs
as Gifts

These original tokens of friendship and affection have a charm all their own. They are also inexpensive to make, so you can please family and friends with generous offerings. Use herbs to create a range of luxuries, from fragrant soaps and pampering bath sachets to scented flower waters and inks, as well as to decorate gift boxes themselves. Whatever the occasion, you can rest assured that your package of herbs will always be well-received.

SOAP ON A ROPE

*Taking pure, unscented soap and perfuming or decorating it
yourself means that you can choose unusual scents and
give the soaps as original gifts.*

*I*N THE DAYS BEFORE forks were much used for dining, soap was supplied in the form of a hard, roughly shaped ball. This was a natural progression from bowls of rose and herb water, which were once brought to the table at the conclusion of every meal.

In India I saw pots and pans being washed with a mixture of wood ash and water, a liquid known in medieval times as lye, which was mixed with melted animal fat and allowed to cool to produce a basic soap. Fragrant herbs and oils were added to the concoction to perfume it. The soap was either formed into rough spheres when the mixture had hardened, or the fresh liquid soap was poured into molds to produce bars. These were then left in the sun and turned each day until they were completely dry.

The technique used here requires no wood ash or fat, so it is a much less messy way of making soap. I use bars of unscented pure soap, but you can use a bar colored in a shade appropriate to your chosen herb, or you can add a drop or two of food coloring instead. You can also fragrance your soap by adding just a couple of drops of essential oil, which has the advantage of making the soap mixture more malleable before you mold it. *Caution:* Be careful when handling essential oils—they are very strong and can affect sensitive skins.

HERB USED
*1 teaspoon of dried rosemary,
very finely crumbled*

Dried rosemary
(*Rosmarinus
officinalis*)

*A selection of herb soaps are suspended
from natural jute ropes, allowing them
to dry out after the bath or shower.
Rosemary is combined with fine
oatmeal to give a fragrant and
mildly exfoliating wash.*

MAKING THE HERBAL SOAP ON A ROPE

For each soap ball you will need: bar of unscented pure soap; metal cheese grater; glass bowl; teaspoon; wooden spoon; 20in (50cm) length of jute rope; and a teaspoon of oatmeal. These soaps only need a small quantity of dried herbs, which must be very finely crushed. Fine oatmeal also acts as an excellent and totally natural, yet gentle, exfoliant, ideal for slightly oily or combination skins. If you find the mixture too dry and difficult to blend (more likely if you have included the oatmeal), carefully add more hot water, a teaspoon at a time, until all the ingredients all come together in a ball.

1 Using the coarse side of an ordinary metal cheese grater, grate the unscented soap bar into a glass bowl. Next, crumble the dried rosemary into manageable pieces, enough for a teaspoonful for each bar of soap.

2 Add the crumbled dried herb, and a teaspoon of oatmeal if desired, to the grated soap in the bowl. Mix 2 or 3 drops of essential oil (I used lavender oil to combine with the rosemary) with a table-spoon of hot water and add to the mixture.

3 Use your hands to mix and combine the dried herbs, oat-meal, and grated soap thoroughly. The hot water will have softened the mixture, but if it does not form easily into a ball, add more hot water, a teaspoon at a time. Be careful not to make the mixture too wet, because this will result in a slack mix that is difficult and sticky to handle.

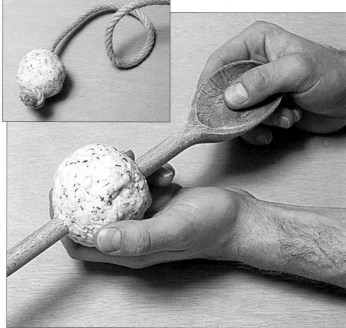

4 When the soap mixture is completely combined, use your hands to form it into a ball. If you want to hang it on a rope, pierce the ball with the handle of a wooden spoon. Leave to dry for several days, turning occasionally so the soap dries evenly. Once the soap has dried out, after 3-4 days, carefully remove the wooden spoon to leave a central hole. Thread through a piece of rope and tie a knot in one end to secure it.

Transparent Herb Soaps

Shiny and smooth, like jewels or ice, these transparent, fragrant soaps each feature a spice or a leaf or sprig of herb captured inside. All kinds of containers and molds may be used, and you can have great fun experimenting with the different effects you can achieve. I have used commercially available molds from bakery suppliers, and also an ice-cube-making tray. Unscented and uncolored glycerine is sold by most good art and craft stores, or you can use glycerine soap bars sold in pharmacies.

A selection of herbs have been captured in these clear glycerine soaps. Ice cube molds shaped like shells are used to make the lavender and clove soaps, and commercial soap molds have been used for the larger soaps, containing cinnamon, lavender, and bay.

1 Grease the mold with vegetable or olive oil. Heat the soap over a double boiler until it melts, add your chosen essential oils to give fragrance, and pour into mold until half-full. Leave to set.

2 Place a bay leaf on top of the first layer of soap, reheat the soap, stirring to prevent a skin from forming on top, and then fill up the mold. Leave to set before removing the soap.

BATH SACHETS

As a change from conventional bath salts, make your own no-sew herbal bath sachets.

For a luxurious soak, use these sachets to infuse the water with the wonderful scent of herbs.

They make delightful welcoming gifts for guests or for your partner at the end of a long day.

*T*HERE IS NO ONE recipe for these wonderful bath sachets; the ingredients can be adapted to suit individual tastes. One suggestion can be found in Ben Jonson's *Volpone* (Act 3, Scene 2)—harking back to a mythical age, it is a rather fantastic formula which is, perhaps, a little too elaborate for my taste:

> *"Thy baths shall be the juice of July-flowers,*
> *Spirits of Roses, and of violets,*
> *The milk of unicorns, and panthers' breath*
> *Gathered in bags and mixed with Cretan wines."*

When making these bath sachets, it is extravagant and impractical to use anything other than a double thickness of cheesecloth or muslin. If you use a ribbon to tie them, make sure it is colorfast—generally I prefer to use cream-colored string.

For delightfully fragranced bath water, simply steep the sachets in warm water for several minutes before bathing. After the refreshing herbs have infused the water, the sachet can be hung from the faucet until your next bath. Each sachet can be used at least three or four times.

Keep the bath sachets, including any that have been used and subsequently dried, in a pretty bowl in the bathroom, making them decorative as well as practical.

MAKING THE BATH SACHETS

Making these sachets requires no sewing at all. Each sachet uses a 13in (33cm) square of muslin or doubled cheesecloth, and an 11in (28cm) piece of cord, string, or colorfast ribbon. Use a shell, with a hole pierced or drilled in it, for decoration if you wish. To fill the sachets, break up the herbs into fairly small pieces and, if desired, add a handful of oatmeal for extra bulk. Mix all the ingredients in a ceramic or glass bowl before placing on the fabric.

HERBS AND SPICES USED

To fill approximately six sachets:
2oz (55g) dried lavender flowers
1oz (30g) diced, dried lemon peel
4 dried bay leaves, crumbled
4 sprigs dried rosemary, crushed
1oz (30g) dried lemon grass, chopped

1 Place a handful of the well-mixed herbs in the center of the square of muslin or cheesecloth. Remove any larger pieces that may puncture the fabric.

2 Gather up the four corners and the edges, then secure the sachet with the cord, tied tightly with a double knot. Allow for a loop so the bag can be hung up when not in use, and tie again, adding the drilled shell for decoration if you wish.

Dried lavender flowers
(Lavandula angustifolia)

Dried lemon peel
(Citrus limon)

Dried rosemary
(Rosmarinus officinalis)

Dried bay leaves
(Laurus nobilis)

Dried lemon grass
(Cymbopogon citratus)

FLOWER WATER

Fragrant herbal flower waters look as wonderful as they smell when subtle combinations of aromatic herbs and colorful flowers are presented in elegant bottles and bowls.

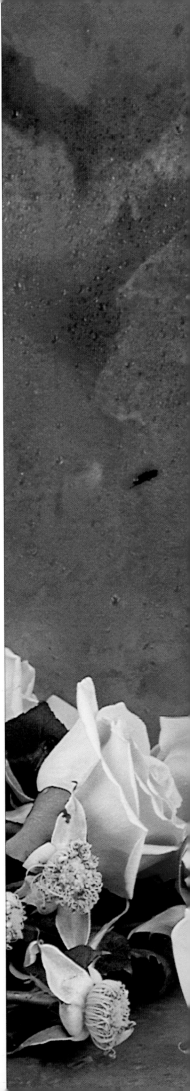

*I*N MEDIEVAL TIMES, it was a common custom among the ruling classes to wash their hands in rosewater at the end of each meal. In the days before cutlery, a large bowl or basin holding herb-scented water was brought to the table, more out of necessity than daintiness. Flower waters were also sprinkled on favored family members and guests as a sign of welcome. Victorian and Edwardian ladies used flower water as a reviving face wash, with the herbs and flowers contributing beneficial essential oils and a gentle fragrance that was much more subtle than many of the synthetic perfumes used today.

These cool flower waters are still wonderfully refreshing as a face and hand wash, and they make lovely scented gifts, especially when presented in pretty glass bottles. They can also be added to a bath, although their subtle fragrance may be too gentle to be noticed—a few drops of essential oils will increase the aroma. In the recipes on pages 88-89, fresh herbs are used, but dried herbs are also effective, because their perfume is concentrated. *Caution:* These waters are purely for external use and should never be ingested.

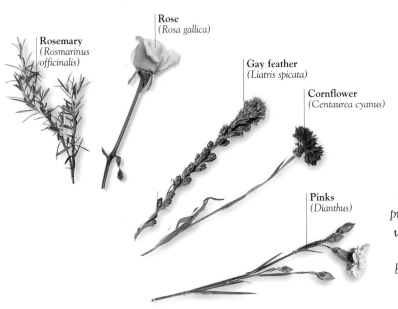

Rosemary
(*Rosmarinus officinalis*)

Rose
(*Rosa gallica*)

Gay feather
(*Liatris spicata*)

Cornflower
(*Centaurea cyanus*)

Pinks
(*Dianthus*)

HERBS USED

3 sprigs rosemary

3 roses

1oz (30g) dried rose petals

2 stems of gay feather

4 cornflowers

6 pinks

Flower waters stored in pretty bottles are an enchanting way to retain the heady scents of summer. These slender bottles would look good in the kitchen or bathroom.

MAKING HERBAL FLOWER WATER

In addition to the herbs, you will need: large glass jar; thin wooden skewer; 1fl oz (35ml) fragance-free alcohol, such as vodka; 4fl oz (150ml) distilled water; glass measuring jug; decorative glass bottle; and food coloring (optional).

It is best to use distilled water, because it has no impurities, and fragrance-free alcohol, as it does not interfere with the scents of the herbs (vodka, the cheapest available, is ideal). If you do not have fresh herbs on hand, you can steep dried herbs in the alcohol instead—their fragrance is concentrated and the herbs are later discarded so you do not need to worry about their appearance.

Before you begin, it is essential that all the equipment you use is thoroughly cleaned, as the slightest speck of dirt may cause bacteria to form, resulting in some very undesirable scented water.

1 Sterilize a large glass jar with a wide top. Measure in 1fl oz (35ml) of fragrance-free alcohol, then add 2fl oz (70ml) of distilled water and mix. Add the herbs and flower heads.

3 Strain the mixture into a glass measuring jug and dilute with 2fl oz (70ml) of distilled water. Add a couple of drops of food coloring if wished. Pour into a sterilized bottle.

4 If you wish, you can decorate your flower water with sprigs of fresh herbs, such as rosemary and geranium. Use robust herbs, as fragile ones will deteriorate more quickly.

2 Drop the roses, gay feather, cornflowers, and pinks into the jar and immerse. Cover the jar securely, and leave the mixture to soften in a cool, dark place for about 5 days.

Lavender and Ginger Water

A small quantity of flower water poured into a wide bowl and filled up with a little warm water will gently scent a room and will look pretty. My recipe for lavender and ginger water is ideal because both lavender and ginger have quite potent smells. For this recipe, use 2fl oz (70ml) vodka, 4fl oz (150ml) distilled water, a handful of dried lavender heads, and two slices of fresh ginger root. Steep the lavender and ginger root in the vodka, diluted with 2fl oz (70ml) distilled water, for three days. Then strain and discard the herbs. Dilute the liquid with the remaining 2fl oz (70ml) of distilled water. Add a couple of drops of amber food coloring at this stage if you wish. Pour the scented water into a bottle, adding a sprig or two of fresh or dried lavender for decoration. By adding six drops of lavender oil to this recipe, you can also make a wonderful warming bath essence, perfect for pampering yourself during long winter months.

5 Wipe the neck of the bottle with a clean, dry cloth and seal with a stopper. Corked bottles are ideal, because any fermentation pressure will be released gradually.

A glass bowl is filled with fragrant lavender and ginger water, decorated with rose petals, and placed on a table near an open window. The subtle scents gently fill the candlelit room.

HERBAL INKS

A deeply romantic idea from days gone by, an infusion of fresh or dried herbs is added to ink,

which can then be used to write fragrant letters to a loved one. Combined with lovely sta-

tionery and a fountain pen, this makes a thoughtful gift for a letter-writing friend.

ONE OF THE sadnesses of our computer-aided and word-processed lives is the fact that the art of letter-writing by hand is all but dead. These days the fax, telephone, and e-mail connect us immediately to those with whom we might previously have corresponded by post. Indeed, it is hard to believe that, once upon a time, an invitation to dinner would have been sent, received, and responded to by hand-delivered letter—all within the day on which you would have been invited to attend.

Originally a medieval notion, scented inks were greatly revived during Victorian times, when they became an important part of a lady's writing paraphernalia, together with a selection of fragranced notepaper and envelopes. Such equipment was used in the daily round of correspondence with lovers and friends, and had great significance when used for love letters. As each flower had its own symbolic meaning within the courtly language of romance, the scent chosen for a particular missive would have conveyed its own message. Lavender, for example, stood for silence and was often used when exchanging secrets. Mint symbolized wisdom, ideal if writing to give a friend advice, and rosemary represented remembrance, which made it an appropriate choice when sending a letter of condolence. Basil and rose signified love, while pansies were associated with love and courtship.

Many varieties of herbs are suitable for fragrancing inks and because they are used as infusions, dried herbs are often better than fresh, since their essential oils are more concentrated. You do not need to worry about looking for pretty flower heads or leaves—even the most woody and unattractive leaves and stems are ideal for this project and, once boiled, yield excellent results.

HERBS USED

15 sprigs of lavender

15 sprigs of rosemary

Lavender
(*Lavandula angustifolia* 'Hidcote')

Rosemary
(*Rosmarinus officinalis*)

MAKING THE HERBAL INKS

It is essential that you use an enamel or glass saucepan for this recipe, as any other type of pan will taint the infusion. It is also wise to reserve a pan specifically for your herbal creations, as it may retain some of the scents and impart these flavors into your next batch of soup.

In addition to the enamel or glass saucepan, you will need: fine-mesh strainer; glass or ceramic bowl; and a bottle of ink in your desired color.

If you are feeling very romantic and creating a rose and lemon grass blend, you can use a pink or red ink to enhance the idea of affection.

1 Place the sprigs of fresh or dried lavender and rosemary into the saucepan. Pour in half a pint of water. Place the pan over a high heat and keep the mixture on a boil until the liquid has reduced by about half.

What could be more romantic than to receive a letter from a loved one that has been gently perfumed by rosemary and lavender?
If giving the ink to a friend, you can present it with an ink pen and a bundle of notepaper, tied with a silk ribbon and embellished with a small bunch of dried lavender.

2 Let the mixture cool, then strain it into a ceramic or glass bowl through a fine-mesh strainer. Return the infusion to the pan, and bring it to a boil again. Carefully watch the pan and reduce the mixture to one generous tablespoonful.

3 Place the pan on one side to cool. Measure three generous tablespoons of ink into a bottle or inkwell and pour the infusion into the ink. Close the lid on the bottle and gently invert it a few times to mix the infusion and ink.

EDIBLE HERB POSY

This fresh herb posy is flat at the back and full at the front, designed to hang on the kitchen wall,

where it will look lovely and be handy for cooking, as all the herbs

arranged in it are edible.

ANY COMBINATION of fresh or dried herbs is ideal for this project, in which the textures and shapes of the different leaves play a major decorative role. All the herbs used in my posy are edible, and a combination of all or even some of these would create a delicious bouquet garni. Of course, the herbs do not have to be used for gastronomic purposes—a posy could be a purely decorative and fragrant present.

If you grow your own herbs in the garden, by the middle of summer you may find you have many more than you can use, or more than you want to put aside for drying, and the posy is a splendid way of using them. The posy would make a welcome present for an avid cook without a garden, and you can make it as large or as small as you like, depending on your supply of fresh herbs.

MAKING THE EDIBLE HERB POSY

In addition to the herbs, you will need: sharp scissors or a knife; some string or twine.

Take your most robust stem first, such as rosemary, to use as the base for the design. The string or twine is attached to this first stem and everything else is bound onto it. As each additional herb is incorporated, preferably in small clumps rather than as single stems, another turn or two of string will hold it in place.

Finer or smaller herbs, such as chives, need to be added in fairly bold groupings so they are not overshadowed by their chunkier neighbors. It is also a good idea to position the more fragile varieties in among the firmer, woody-stemmed herbs, because this will give them protection and support.

HERBS USED
20 sprigs each of:
rosemary, parsley, bay,
chives, and sage

Bay
(*Laurus nobilis*)

Parsley
(*Petroselinum crispum*)

Sage
(*Salvia officinalis*)

Rosemary
(*Rosmarinus officinalis*)

Chives
(*Allium schoenoprasum*)

1 Make sure that all your herbs are prepared. Clean off any damaged leaves and remove side shoots and lower branches to leave a good length of stem.

Bound and tied with twine, the posy makes a simple and unusual gift—especially when wrapped in brown paper, which sets off the vibrant greens of the herbs.

2 Attach a length of twine to a base stem of rosemary, about two-thirds from its tip. Bind a cluster of parsley onto it in a couple of turns of twine.

3 Insert a stem or two of bay and bind in the same way. Cross the remaining parsley, sage, and chive stems at angles to give structure to the posy.

GIFT BOXES

*These attractive boxes are an appropriate way to give presents that contain herbs,
such as potpourri, soaps, and bath sachets. But there's really no limit to what
you can put in them—and they even make lovely gifts on their own.*

THERE ARE SO MANY wonderful boxes and
containers available these days that you can find
a shape or size to suit just about any gift. Boxes
are also extremely useful for those awkwardly shaped
presents that are so time-consuming to wrap. By adding a
pretty herbal decoration to these purchased boxes you can
make even the simplest and most humble of presents look
extra special.

The plainer the box or wrapping paper, the better
because the natural herb decoration will stand out more
effectively against a neutral background. There are two
methods of securing the herbs to the boxes: you can either
use a small dollop of glue (see Techniques, page 100) or
string or twine. Even simple yarn or embroidery thread ties
can look extremely effective.

The boxes themselves are often expensive, so it is worth
looking out for any containers that can be recycled. Many
household items are sold in boxes, as well as apparel, such
as shoes, ties, or scarves. Covered in pretty paper or fabric,
these too make ideal gift boxes.

HERBS USED
1 small and 2 large bay leaves

Bay
(Laurus nobilis)

*A bow of fresh bay leaves
decorates the pierced lid of a
simple cardboard box, making
an ideal and inexpensive way
to present and store potpourri
or another scented gift.*

MAKING THE BAY BOW

In addition to bay leaves, you will need: a glue gun and container of your choice. Make sure that you use young leaves because they are more pliable. If you do not have any bay leaves, you could experiment with other leafy herbs that dry well, such as sage.

A variation on this theme is to just use glue to stick single bay leaves, or your chosen herbs, onto the top of your gift box to form a motif. Another idea that works well is to make a feature of the herbs on the sides of the boxes. On one of the circular containers (shown on p. 95), for example, I have overlapped the bay leaves at both ends to create a ring around the middle of the box. Flower heads could also be used this way, but make sure that they are fairly flat and will not shed their petals once they dry out.

1 For each box choose two large, unmarked bay leaves, both approximately 3in (7cm) long, and one slightly smaller leaf for your decoration.

2 Take one of the larger leaves and, using the glue gun, put a dab of glue at the base of the back of the leaf. Fold the top of the leaf over to secure.

3 Glue the other large leaf in the same way and join the two tips together with glue.

4 Wrap the small leaf round the middle to conceal the join, trimming it to size, then gluing. Glue the bow, so the joined middle is hidden, onto the center of the top of the box.

Posy-wrapped gift box

Another effective way of decorating a box is to make up a small posy of herbs and attach it with ribbon or cord. Here, I have used fresh safflower with goldenrod. These are robust, flowering herbs which will not shrivel or wilt if allowed to dry on a gift box. A length of jute cord has been used to secure this little posy on top of the box. A combination of lavender and rosemary also looks charming, or you can use a single fresh or dried peony. You could also experiment with other fairly sturdy herbs, such as eryngium, eucalyptus, or globe thistles.

Extremely simple to make, this little decorative posy turns an ordinary gift box into something really special. What better way to show someone you care than by adding such a thoughtful finishing touch?

1 Assemble a small posy of goldenrod and safflower. Use approximately 3 small stems of each herb, crossing the stems to form the posy.

2 Wire around the stems to secure then and tie the posy onto the gift box with jute cord.

Techniques
with Herbs

There are a few basic skills and techniques that every decorative herb artist needs to have. Here, advice is given on the harvesting of fresh flowers and herbs and the best ways of drying and storing them so that they last for years and retain their fragrance. The mechanics of wiring flowers is explained, as are techniques that can make all the difference to the presentation of herbal gifts.

GETTING STARTED

HERE IS VERY little specialized equipment required to make the projects in this book. With a little ingenuity you may be able to find and adapt much of it from what you already have around the house. There are, however, a few things that are essential to any herb decorative artist. A pair of good sharp scissors, preferably of the type used by florists, are your primary tool and are a good investment because they will last for years and can be resharpened as necessary. Florist's wires—stub wire and reel wire—are also materials that you really can't do without. These items need to be stored properly in a toolbox or drawer. Florist's wire is untreated and will rust if it gets damp. The more types of decorative projects you tackle, the more equipment you will accumulate, and here I illustrate the items that I have found to be the essential tools of my trade.

BASIC EQUIPMENT

Equipment is not very expensive. It is useful to have all these items at hand when starting a project, as together they will accommodate most decorative situations. A glue gun is a good investment—you can apply glue accurately without any mess. All you need now are the herbs and spices of your choice.

USING A GLUE GUN

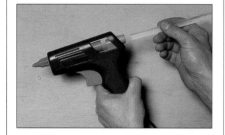

1 Here, a pliable, rigid glue stick is slotted into the gun.

2 When plugged in, the heat element softens the glue. The trigger is pressed to release the glue.

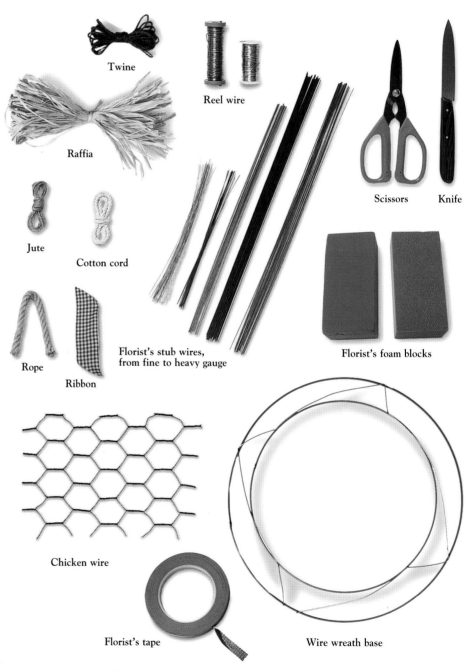

Twine

Reel wire

Raffia

Scissors   Knife

Jute

Cotton cord

Rope

Ribbon

Florist's stub wires, from fine to heavy gauge

Florist's foam blocks

Chicken wire

Florist's tape

Wire wreath base

WIRING

*W*IRING DRIED OR fresh plants is not difficult, but takes practice to do it quickly and well. I remember well my first attempts and how clumsy I felt. Eventually, you will be able to wire all kinds of fresh and dried herbs and spices as proficiently as any expert. One of the biggest mistakes people make is to use the wrong size of wire—either too thick or too thin, depending on the stem or plant. Florist's wires, also known as stub wires, can be bought in a number of different thicknesses, referred to as gauges.

The higher the number of a wire, the thicker it will be—medium-gauge wire is the thickest you will need for any of the projects in the book. For very delicate stems, use the finest gauge of wire; for most herbs, use medium-gauge wire; and for heavy construction work, or the thickest, toughest stems, use heavy-gauge wire. All the different sizes of wire, available in a variety of lengths (see opposite), are easy to find in a florist's supply store, and it is useful to have a number of different thicknesses available as you work.

WIRING LARGE STEMS

It is much easier to wire and attach large or thick-stemmed herbs if you deal with them individually. Generally, medium-gauge wire is used for these thick stems, although you might need to use the heavier-gauge wire for very tough stems (heavy-gauge wire is really only used for securing large architectural projects, such as wall hangings and herb wreaths). You will find it easiest to push the wire through a thick stem by cutting the tip of it to a point and holding the stem as near to the point as possible before pushing it firmly through. Make sure you push the wire through the center of each stem (see right).

1 Push the thick stub wire through the stem end of the garlic.

2 Bend the wire ends to form a "hairpin," twisting one over the other.

WIRING BUNCHES

The weight of the stems or flower heads dictates the width of wire used for bunches of herbs. It is a good idea to wire all the components of your project before you start.

1 Arrange your bunch of dried herbs and trim stems to one length. Bend a 12in (30cm) stub wire into a "hairpin" and place over the middle of the stems.

2 Bend one end of the wire around the stems and over the other end. Turn the wire around the stems two or three times and bring the ends together.

WIRING LEAVES

Firm and fleshy leaves, such as bay, are ideal for covering shapes and spheres. They are easy to attach to such bases using a small loop of wire or a pin. Push the ends of a wire "hairpin" through the middle of the top side of a leaf, into the herb decoration.

HARVESTING & DRYING

*T*HE HARVESTING AND drying of herbs is an art in itself. Timing is critical—although blooms left in a vase may dry out on their own and still look attractive, flowers and herbs really need to be harvested at the right time if they are to last and look their best. This involves judging the cutting time accurately and harvesting the flowers up to 24 hours before they reach their peak and bloom fully. Once cut, they will still continue to open as they use up the remaining sap in their stems.

Alternatively, you could cut the flowers earlier, put them into a bucket of water, and then remove them for drying at just the right moment. Harvesting and drying herbs and flowers you have grown yourself at home is the best option

because you can judge more easily when they are at the best stage of their development. If you buy herbs from retail stores or wholesalers to take home and dry, you run the risk of purchasing less-than-perfect blooms, which will look brown and unsightly when they dry out. It would be unfortunate to go to all that expense only to see the herbs end up in a bowl of potpourri.

The basic techniques of drying herbs given here are easy to master, needing only a little time and care. It is best to dry herbs immediately after harvesting—the herbs retain more color and shape that way. The finer details, however, come with experience: you will find out just how long to leave plants hanging through trial and error.

HARVESTING FLOWERS
Here are summer blooms from the garden, harvested for drying and preserving (left). Flowers are best collected in dry weather around noon and after any dew has evaporated. They should be left spread out in open containers until they are ready to be dried, as they bruise very easily.

POTS OF HERBS
Herbs for drying can easily be harvested from pots of herbs grown on the kitchen windowsill. Pick only healthy, whole leaves with no blemishes, and treat the leaves gently.

 Thyme

 Parsley

 Basil

 Rosemary

AIR-DRYING HERBS

The easiest way to dry herbs and flowers is just to hang them upside down in the air in any available warm, dark place. An attic or outdoor shed, where they can stay undisturbed, is ideal, as long as the temperature is constant and the air circulation is good. They will need to hang for a week or so, until they are crisp to the touch. Any remaining moisture will cause the plants to soften and spoil when they are stored.

1 Remove the lowest leaves from the stems of the flowers (here, fresh larkspur). Then fasten a bunch of stems firmly and tightly together with a rubber band. It must be tight enough to allow for the shrinking of the stems when dry.

2 Make a hook at each end of a length of florist's stub wire. Insert one hook through the bunch of stems held by the rubber band. Hook the other end over a rack or pole and leave for a week or so until completely dried out.

DRYING TIME
An old apple storage rack, hung from wires, makes a good herb drying device. If you are drying different herbs or flowers all at once, group them according to species, as the drying time will vary between plants. It will also be easier to store them if a particular species is kept together. Dry large stems and flower heads individually, rather than in bunches. From left to right, sea holly (Eryngium maritimum), sunflower (Helianthus annuus), purple and white larkspur (Consolida ajacis), and eucalyptus (Eucalyptus gunnii) have just been hung up to dry.

SILICA-GEL DRYING

Flowers and herbs that have heads with many tiny or delicate petals tend to shrivel or collapse if dried in the air, which can be very disappointing. One way to dry such fragile plant material is to use silica-gel crystals, which resemble a fine, sugar-like powder and absorb a great deal of moisture. Delicate flowers or herbs can be buried in an airtight box of silica-gel crystals for several days, until all their moisture has been absorbed by the grains. The crystals are fairly expensive, but can be dried out in the oven and used again; they turn blue when full of moisture and will return to white if slowly dried on a baking sheet.

1 Pour silica-gel crystals into a box with an airtight lid. Place the flower head (here a peony) face up on top.

2 Sprinkle crystals very gently into and around the flower head, being careful not to distort the petals. Keep adding the crystals until the flower is entirely covered.

3 Seal the box with the lid. Leave the flower head buried for at least three days, then very carefully pour off the top layer of the silica-gel grains to reveal the preserved flower. Lift it out gently by hand or with tweezers. If the flower head is not yet dry, repeat the entire drying process.

4 Use a soft artist's paintbrush to gently brush away any grains of silica gel from the delicate petals, then store the flower heads.

MICROWAVE DRYING

You can also use a microwave to dry flowers, and this method has the advantage of keeping the colors bright and strong. The one drawback of the microwave is that the petals tend to shrivel as a result of being starved of moisture so quickly. Microwaves will also dry herbs without affecting their flavor, but may diminish their therapeutic properties. Dry petals in a microwave for one minute, then check; if more time is needed, dry the petals at 10-second intervals.

OTHER DRYING METHODS

The easiest way to dry large numbers of petals for potpourri is to spread them out on a sheet of newspaper and leave them in a dry and sunny room. If they are turned a couple of times a day, they will dry out relatively quickly. You can use this method for drying some whole flowers and bunches of herbs, too. This method works well for sage, chives, and helichrysum leaves. When drying bunches of herbs on newspaper, choose herbs that are fairly delicate—thick-stemmed plants are best dried by the air-drying method.

STORAGE

STORING YOUR dried flowers and herbs may seem like the least complicated part of the process, but it is essential to do it right if you don't want the beautiful products of your labors to become moldy. Flowers and herbs to be used in decorations are best stored in cardboard boxes, whereas potpourri ingredients should be stored in airtight glass containers. All boxed dried herbs and flowers should be kept in a dry, dark, cool place where the temperature is constant and air circulates well. It is useful to label all your packages and containers so you know what is in each one. Glass containers help you see at a glance which stocks are running low. However, they must be stored away from direct sunlight because it fades the colors of the contents and reduces the perfume.

A DRIED HERB STORE

The wide-necked, airtight jars and bottles shown here are ideal for storing potpourri petals, buds, and spices. The folded-over paper bags, secured with clothespins, are used to store pods, cones, and completed pomanders.

STORING HERBS IN A TISSUE-LINED BOX

A simple cardboard box—but one with rigid sides and a good, secure lid—is ideal for storing bunches of dried herbs. A shoe box is perfect for the job and is the right size for many species. A set of standard-sized boxes will make the herbs easy to label and stack together, and will even look attractive. Do not be tempted to store too many bunches in one box because they may become squashed and the shapes of the flower heads and leaves distorted.

LINING WITH TISSUE

The secret of success is to line the boxes with tissue paper and fold the tissue over between layers of stored bunches to protect them all from damage. Use a different box for each variety of plant so the scents do not mingle and become confused.

PRESENTATION

N O MATTER how perfectly you have made up your project, and how beautifully you have dried your herbs, the effect can all be lost if the final presentation is poor. The finishing touches shown here are just some of many you could create yourself, but they call for some very useful skills. Making a really good bow is a craft worth learning. There is nothing more enjoyable than receiving a beautifully wrapped bouquet or posy that has been finished with flamboyant silk or paper ribbon and

a matching ribbon bow. Burlap is a fashionable and understated alternative material, and its rough texture combines well with that of dried herbs. Along with the bow shown opposite, you can also make a burlap bottom piece for a wall hanging (see pp. 40-43) by doubling up a tube of burlap, bunching it together in the middle with wire, and tying on another piece of burlap to hide the wire. The piece can be attached to the bottom of a wall hanging with wire "hairpins" or with glue.

MAKING A RIBBON BOW

This beautiful bow which decorates a posy of fresh or dried herbs is not actually tied from the same piece of ribbon that binds the posy together, but is specially designed using a separate piece of ribbon formed into a series of loops.

Once the loops are secured and the bow designed, it is tied or pinned into place to look as if it is an integral part of the posy. The fact that it can be removed and reused is an advantage.

1 Use a length of ribbon about 20in (50cm) long and wide enough for your posy. Leaving a tail of about 5in (12cm) at one end, pinch and gather the ribbon into a series of loops.

2 Stop bunching when you have a total of four loops, two on each side. The remaining length of ribbon will make another tail, corresponding to the 5in (12cm) length left at the start.

3 Now twist a good length of heavy-gauge florist's wire around the gathered middle to secure the loops of the bow. Pull out the loops to arrange them attractively.

4 Cut a second piece of ribbon of the same design to a length of 12in (30cm). Tie this neatly over the wire in the middle to cover it. This will also end in tails, adding to the effect.

5 The finished bow is now ready to be attached to a posy. If you omit the wire from making the bow, the bow could be used to secure an ordinary gift wrapping.

MAKING A BURLAP BOW

Burlap can be substituted with another material, perhaps one that coordinates with a room's furnishings. By cutting from material, the bow can be as large as you like. This large bow is made from a piece of burlap measuring 36in (90cm) square.

2 On the seamless side, gather the fabric together in the middle, holding the loose ends behind. Secure the loose ends by looping stub wire around the middle and twisting at the back.

1 Cut the burlap to the required size for your bow. Fold the two sides, then the two ends to the center.

3 If you feel that the loops of your bow are not plump enough, tweak them into position at this halfway stage.

4 Cut a second, narrow strip of fabric, turn under its raw edges, and tie it around the middle of the bow to hide the wire.

5 The bow is now complete, ready to be attached to a garland or swag.

BOTTLES WITH A DIFFERENCE

Bath oils and flower and herb waters make attractive gifts when decorated imaginatively. As you look around at the materials you have available, use your imagination to create unusual and eye-catching effects.

Here a corked bottle of flower water is given a finishing touch by adding a scented geranium leaf.

Curl the scented geranium leaf down over the cork and secure with string. Wrap around the cork twice and tie with a simple knot.

IMAGINATIVE BOTTLES
The leaf-topped bottle stands beside one that is prettily decorated with dried lavender and a slice of dried orange.

Directory of Herbs & Spices

Herbs are fragrant plants of which the leaves, stems, flowers, seeds, and roots are used fresh or dried for mildly flavoring dishes or for medicinal purposes. Spices are also used in food and medicine but they are much stronger and only come from dried parts—the seeds, flowers, leaves, bark, or roots—of aromatic, usually tropical, plants. Both herbs and spices are used decoratively; all those you need are detailed in this section.

DECORATIVE HERBS

The following pages provide an introduction to the best decorative herbs—they are listed alphabetically by Latin name, and the entries detail the different characteristics and uses of each herb.

ACHILLEA MILLEFOLIUM
YARROW
An invasive plant, 12-36in (30-90cm) in height, which spreads via its prolific root system. Yarrow can almost take over in the herb garden, and so it should be grown in a container. Its blooms are borne on tallish stems covered with fairly insignificant, feathery green leaves, and are made up of tiny, daisy-like flowers in mauve, lilac, or white. Mauve ones are best for drying because they retain color, while the white ones dry to a brownish shade. Use for sculptural decorations, such as herb pomanders and topiary.

ALCHEMILLA MOLLIS
LADY'S MANTLE
A huge favorite everywhere, alchemilla reminds me of rambling country gardens. Its gentle, bushy habit softens the edges of paths and borders. It grows to a height of 6-20in (15-50cm) and its enveloping, citrus-green, scallop-edged leaves give it its common name. Clusters of the graceful, very small green flowers are wonderful fresh or dried, and suit small-scale herbal decorations. The leaves are excellent in potpourri, and both leaves and flowers can be used in swags and garlanded baskets. Harvest them once the flowers have started to open, and dry in bunches, hanging them upside down in a warm, dark place.

ALLIUM
CHIVES (*A. schoenoprasum*)
This herb grows to 8-12in (20-30cm) tall and has mauve flowers in midsummer. It is known by the French as *petit poireau*, literally meaning "little leek," and its smell, taste, and appearance do indeed resemble the leek. For this reason, it is best suited to culinary and decorative uses, such as herb posies and edible centerpieces. Once dried, it shrivels and becomes as anonymous as lawn cuttings.
GARLIC (*A. sativum*), which grows to a height of 12-18in (30-45cm), has been cultivated for many thousands of years and much mythology still surrounds it. In isolated parts of eastern Europe, some village funerals still feature open coffins filled with garlic to ward off evil spirits. The edible bulbs make wonderful decorations because of their unusual color—the individual cloves are covered with a thin, tissue-paper-like, whitish layer, often with touches of purple. The bulbs dry out perfectly, but need to be wired while they are still fresh. They have a strong, distinctive aroma even when dried, making them only suitable for culinary decorations, such as a kitchen wall hanging.

ALOYSIA TRIPHYLLA
(SYN. *LIPPIA CITRIODORA*)
LEMON VERBENA
This herb is native to South and Central America and was introduced into other parts of the world by the Spaniards. It can grow to 12ft (4m) tall, but being frost-tender, may be half that size in northern climates. Its leaves have impressive lasting qualities—they retain their lemon fragrance for years, which makes them the perfect ingredient for a wide range of aromatic projects, such as potpourri, bath bags, and scented pillows. They are also excellent for herbal teas and infusions.

ANETHUM GRAVEOLENS
DILL
This hardy annual grows wild as a weed in North and South America. It grows to 24in (60cm) tall, and looks much like fennel, with soft, feathery green leaves that are rather delicate—when dried, it is best to use the leaves only in sachets or scented pillows. Its hollow stems are more robust and may be used fresh or dried for herb-wrapped glasses or in bundles for garlanded baskets. Fresh dill is perfect for edible table centerpieces and its seed heads may be dried—these look spectacular placed in potpourri or as part of a garland or herb wreath.

ANGELICA ARCHANGELICA
ANGELICA

This plant is naturalized in cooler European countries and North America—in all, over 30 different varieties exist. It is a large plant that grows to a height of 3-8ft (1-2.5m). Its leaves, seeds, and, unusually, its roots are delicately perfumed, and are especially useful in bath bags, scented pillows, and potpourri. The flower and seed heads may be dried and used whole in decorations or crumbled in other aromatic projects.

ANTHRISCUS CEREFOLIUM
CHERVIL

This hardy annual herb, which grows to a height 10-15in (25-38cm), has tiny white clusters of flowers in late spring or summer and delicate, feathery green leaves that look a little like parsley. Chervil is excellent grown in containers, including windowboxes, as it thrives in shady areas. It works particularly well when planted among other edible herbs, such as mint and parsley. It has the added benefit of retaining its leaves throughout the winter months. The leaves, which have a slight aniseed taste, dry easily, retaining a delicate flavor and a faint scent.

AQUILEGIA VULGARIS
COLUMBINE

This elegant and delightful flowering herb grows to 12-24in (30-60cm) tall, and is popular for country gardens. Its flowers, which appear in late spring through to midsummer, are white, purple, and blue—they have oddly shaped tubular petals with long curved tips. It is excellent as a cut flower for using with other herbs on a flowering wreath or in a

EDIBLE TABLE CENTERPIECE
This simple arrangement (see p. 21), combining the vibrant greens and contrasting textures of rosemary, parsley, and dill, makes a stunning focus for a summer lunch.

tussie-mussie. Alternatively, its dried flower heads can also make an unusual addition to potpourri, where the flowers' shapes may be seen to best advantage. Its seed heads dry well and have an interesting shape.

ARTEMISIA
SOUTHERNWOOD (A. abrotanum)

The genus *Artemisia* contains several aromatic herbs which all grow to heights between 24in-4ft (60cm-1.2m). Southernwood grows wild in Italy and Spain and is known as European wormwood. The delicate gray-green leaves are soft and almost fluffy in appearance—a great asset in the garden. It has a fairly distinctive and pungent aroma—sprigs of it were worn by women going to church in the hope that its heady scent would keep them awake during long and boring sermons! Insects hate its scent, hence its inclusion in moth bags, and its use among linens. For this

reason the French refer to it as *garderobe*, meaning literally "keeper of clothes."

WORMWOOD (A. absinthium) is a similar foliage plant to southernwood, again with a very distinctive scent. It is wonderful in fresh arrangements and is easily air-dried. Once dried, it may be crumbled and added to mixtures for moth bags or gentlemen's sachets—it has an unusual, unflowery smell. It is also used as a culinary herb in parts of southern Italy, to flavor vermouth and, notoriously, absinthe.

TARRAGON (A. dracunculus) has slender leaves of the same gray-green as its relatives, but its scent is much more palatable. Used in many culinary dishes, it is an appropriate addition to table decorations, such as centerpieces, tray cloths, and napkin rings. When it is dried it can be included in the more robust potpourris and scented sachets. Air-dry it in bunches of no more than three or four stems to allow adequate air circulation. Because its scent is less intense than the other artemesias, it must be stored in an airtight box or jar.

BORAGO OFFICINALIS
BORAGE

Borage is a native of Aleppo, Syria and is naturalized throughout Europe, where it has a long history of being grown for its leaves and pollen-filled, clear blue, star-shaped flowers, from which bees make wonderful honey. It grows to a height of 12-30in (30-75cm) and is an easy plant to propagate from seed. The hairy leaves, which taste vaguely of cucumber, make a wonderful addition to summer fruit punches. Add the immature tips and leaves to a salad, together with the blue flowers for a very pretty effect. The flowers can also be used as decoration on cakes and desserts. Dried, they may be added to potpourri to give a delicate blue accent.

CALENDULA OFFICINALIS
MARIGOLD

This prolific flower will delight anyone's heart—especially if glimpsed on cloudy days. The plant grows to 12-20in (30-50cm) tall and has a distinctive warm scent, which intensifies in the dried flower heads. The bright orange petals were once used to give cheese a brighter color. The flower has been put to many uses throughout the world, such as to decorate Hindu temples and statues in India and for flavoring and adding color to breads and cakes in Europe. Use the petals within gauzy sachets, such as tray cloths or pillows, where their strong color can be seen through the fabric. Dried flower heads also brighten up potpourri.

CARTHAMUS TINCTORIUS
SAFFLOWER, DYER'S SAFFRON

This bright orange flowering herb is also known as bastard saffron because of its use in place of the costly spice saffron (to which it is not related). It grows to a height of 24-36in (60-90cm) and is much cultivated in India, where it is used for dyeing and for culinary purposes—I have seen magnificent fields of it in full flower. Harvest it as soon as the orange petals are beginning to emerge from the green buds and air-dry it in small bunches. Safflower is a very useful decorative herb because, not only does it have an interesting shape, color, and texture, it is also robust and dries well. It can be used in many projects—drop flower heads into potpourri, wire small bunches into wreaths and garlands, or use to add a splash of color to table centerpieces.

CENTAUREA CYANUS
CORNFLOWER

This flower was named after Chiron, a legendary centaur who first taught mankind about the healing properties of herbs. Growing to a height of 12-36in (30-90cm), it has bright blue flowers which are borne on slender, hollow, hairy stems. You can dry the flowers on a flat surface providing you pick them as they burst open and spread them out to encourage plenty of air circulation. Cornflowers are used in herb decorations to add color (but not scent)—dried flower heads enhance potpourri and mixtures for gauzy sachets. Use them fresh in flower water at the distilling stage to add a subtle blue tint.

CHAMAEMELUM NOBILE
(SYN. ANTHEMIS NOBILIS)
CHAMOMILE

A real "Old English" favorite, chamomile has been held in high esteem for over 2,000 years for its importance in Mediterranean-region medicine cabinets. It grows to 12in (30cm) tall, has a creeping habit and flowers with conical golden centers and white petals. When bruised, the leaves smell vaguely of newly mown grass and apples, making it an excellent plant for a scented lawn. The dried leaves and flowers are essential ingredients for pillows or relaxing bath bags because of their soporific properties.

CONSOLIDA AJACIS
LARKSPUR

A relative of the delphinium, this pretty flowering herb is easily grown from seed. It grows to a height of 36in (90cm)—tall spires of pink, white, and blue flowers are borne on stems covered with fluffy, light green leaves. It is used as a cut flower, but remove the leaves which sit below the water line because they quickly make the water foul-smelling. Air-dry in small bunches and use to add color to potpourri or flower pillows and, once wired, to garlands and wreaths.

CONVALLARIA MAJALIS
LILY OF THE VALLEY

Essential in any garden and loved by brides, this delicate and beautiful plant is happy growing in humus-rich, shady soils. Once established, it will quickly form a sizeable patch. This small plant grows to a height of 12in (30cm) and has dainty, waxy white flowers which have a wonderful perfume. The flowers may be dried using silica-gel crystals and then placed among potpourri or wired into wreaths and garlands. Use fresh in tussie-mussies or herb posies—together with thyme and rosemary, it looks as good as any greenhouse-grown flower.

CORIANDRUM SATIVUM
CILANTRO, CORIANDER

This herb has been cultivated as a medicinal and culinary herb for at least 3,000 years and was brought to Europe by the Romans. It is an annual which can grow to 24in (60cm) tall and has flat clusters of white or pinkish flowers from early to mid-summer. With its soft green leaves it looks quite similar to Italian, or flat-leaf, parsley. It is used in culinary dishes because of its unique pungent aroma—it is therefore an excellent choice for inclusion in an edible herb table decoration or salad. Its shiny, round seeds are also quite palatable—they have a subtle, fragrant taste.

CYNARA CARDUNCULUS
CARDOON

This dramatic and statuesque plant, which grows to a height of 3-6ft (1-1.8m), and its larger relation, *C. scolymus*, the edible globe artichoke, take up quite a lot of room so they are not ideal for small gardens. However, if you have room to grow one, use its elegant gray-silver leaves fresh and its bluish-purple, thistle-like flower heads fresh or dried in sculptural decorations, such as garlanded boxes and herb wreaths. Dry the flower heads carefully—either by hanging them upside down in a warm, dark place or by placing them near a radiator and turning daily.

KITCHEN WALL HANGING
Globe artichoke flower heads, with their striking appearance, are wired in with edible herbs and spices, including thyme and garlic, in this handsome piece (see pp. 40-43).

113

HERBAL POTPOURRI

The subtle tones of dried eucalyptus leaves, lavender flower heads, and honesty, combined with a handful of pinks petals, blend beautifully with the silver bowl (see pp. 50-53).

DIANTHUS
PINK

Another favorite garden flower, the *Dianthus* genus actually consists of over 300 hardy and half-hardy species and varieties found in South Africa through to Eurasia and beyond. Growing to 12-36in (30-90cm) tall, they prefer a dry soil and sunny position, where they will flower throughout the summer months. The gently perfumed, salmon-pink flowers can be added to flower waters as decoration at the bottling stage, or used fresh in tussie-mussies, herb posies, and wreaths. The flowers may be dried with care in small bunches using either the silica-gel or air-drying methods. The dried flower heads add an attractive texture and color to potpourri.

CLOVE CARNATION (*D. caryophyllus*) has long been cultivated for its beautiful deep burgundy flowers and subtle fruity perfume. The word carnation comes from the same origin as "coronation"—pinks were used to make garlands and wreaths in ancient Greece to honor the gods. The loose petals can be dried in a microwave, or the complete flower heads can be air- or silica-dried for inclusion in potpourri.

DIGITALIS
FOXGLOVE

One of the most beautiful wild flowers, these spired plants in shades of white to purple love a woodland setting in a rich, loamy soil. They can grow to 3ft (1m) tall and are highly poisonous (parts of the plant are used to make a stimulant drug for heart conditions). Bees adore the tubular, bell-shaped flowers, which develop into wonderful seed pods. Gather them at the end of the summer and air-dry for use in wreaths and wall hangings.

ERYNGIUM MARITIMUM
SEA HOLLY

This herb can occasionally be seen growing wild in exposed conditions, but generally it is regarded as a cultivated plant for the garden. Prickly and very robust, it grows to a height of 36in (90cm) and looks very much like a thistle. When dried its leaves retain their silver and metallic blue-gray colors. The flowers and

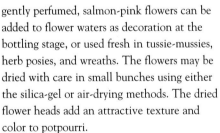

leaves may be used in wreaths and swags, and the flowers also look good combined with silvery eucalyptus and the purple-grays of lavender in potpourri. The roots were once candied and sold as sweetmeats.

EUCALYPTUS GUNNII
EUCALYPTUS

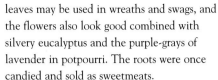

Grown for its beautiful, burnished gray bark and leaves like shiny silver coins, this tree is a native of Australia. Once established, eucalyptus grows exceedingly quickly to a height of 30-80ft (10-25m). Even when dry the leaves contain a strong, invigorating essential oil, which is used in cold cures and decongestants. Used fresh or dried in decorations, the leaves provide good color and add a warm, slightly medicinal scent to garlands, potpourri, and herb-filled sachets.

FILIPENDULA ULMARIA
MEADOWSWEET

Fragrant meadowsweet is a common plant found growing along roadsides throughout the summer months. It grows to 2-4ft (60cm-1.2m) tall and has fluffy, cream flowers with a faint scent of almonds. The flowers were, and still are, used to flavor beer and mead; indeed its name derives from its use in making mead and its use in medieval times as a "strewing" herb to scatter on floors. It is excellent included in sachets, pillows, and potpourri.

FOENICULUM VULGARE
FENNEL

This hardy perennial grows wild around the shores of the Mediterranean (*foeniculum* is derived from the Latin word for hay) and in some areas of North America. Introduced into premedieval England, where it naturalized on the chalky south-coast cliffs, it was used to guard against witchcraft and evil, and was hung above doorways and eaten during Lent. A statuesque plant, which will thrive in open ground or a container, it may grow to 6ft (1.8m) tall. During summer months it has delicate, golden-yellow flower heads, each looking like an umbrella frame without the fabric. Use its soft, feathery foliage in fresh arrangements and, when dried, add its hollow stems, in wired bunches, to potpourri and wreaths. Air-dry in small quantities.

GALIUM
WOODRUFF (*G. odoratum*)
A relative of the tenacious "cleavers," with its hook-covered leaves, this is a good ground-covering plant, which grows to a height of 12in (30cm) and is happy in shade. During early summer the small clusters of green leaves make a dense carpet, which becomes covered with star-shaped flowers in purest white. These fragrant flowers are used in perfume-making, not only for their scent but also as a fixative for other aromas. For this reason, it is an excellent choice for inclusion in potpourri, scented sachets, and flower waters.

LADY'S BEDSTRAW (*G. verum*) has a name which may originate from its use as the filling for wealthy ladies' mattresses in the time of Henry VIII—or just possibly from its supposed inclusion in the hay placed in the manger in Bethlehem. Found growing in fields in Northeast USA, it reaches a height of 12in (30cm) and has clusters of bright yellow flowers running the length of its stems, which have a soothing haylike scent. This scent makes it an essential ingredient for sleep pillows and soothing sachets. Its use in curdling and coloring cheese gives it its alternative name of "cheese rennet."

HELIANTHUS ANNUUS
SUNFLOWER
This annual is a North American native, grown there for some 3,000 years before its introduction into Europe in the sixteenth century. It can be grown from a small seed and reaches a height of 3-10ft (1-3m). Now cultivated as a crop for its oils and seeds, smaller-flowered varieties are available as cut flowers all year round, both fresh and dried. Sunflowers look wonderful when wired into large, architectural arrangements, such as a kitchen wall hangings, garlanded baskets, or brightly colored wreaths.

HELICHRYSUM ITALICUM
CURRY PLANT
If you stand near this plant after heavy rain, it smells very strongly of curry. Widely grown in South Africa, where it is an indigenous herb, it grows to 18in (45cm) tall and its gray-green leaves are slightly hairy and fairly fine. Bright yellow flowers, which look like tiny daisies, are clustered into small flattish heads that dry perfectly and are amazingly robust, maintaining their color for many years. Use its foliage in fresh arrangements and its dried flower heads in gauzy sachets.

HUMULUS LUPULUS
HOP
A relative of the stinging nettle, the hop was used in beer-brewing in northern Europe from early medieval times, but in England it was thought an unwholesome weed and its use was banned by Henry VI and Henry VIII. A perennial, it grows with great rapidity each year to a height of 23ft (7m) and

then dies back—it is the female plants that are cultivated because they bear leafy conical "catkins"– the beer-making parts. Wherever it is grown for brewing you will see it twining up tall wooden structures. Hops have a distinctive smell and are said to be slightly soporific, hence their inclusion in sachets and sleep pillows.

HYSSOPUS OFFICINALIS
HYSSOP
This is an evergreen herb which forms fairly bushy plants that are sometimes used as edgings in knot gardens. It grows to 18in-4ft (45cm-1.2m) tall and its pretty blue flowers are loved by butterflies and bees—the flowers look wonderful used fresh in tussie-mussies or flower arrangements. The flower heads, stems, and leaves all have an aromatic scent, which is distilled by the perfume industry—the oil was once more sought after than lavender oil. Its flowers are fairly insignificant when dried.

IRIS
YELLOW FLAG (*I. pseudacorus*) grows to a height of 36in-5ft (90cm-1.5m) and is native to Europe. Its flowers grow in clusters of two or three buds per stem and its leaves, springing straight from the rhizome, are broad and flat. The word "flag" comes from the perianth petals in the middle of each bloom, which flutter in the wind. The iris is the *fleur-de-lys* of French royalty; the three petals represent valor, wisdom, and faith. As well as the fresh flower heads, the seed heads are also decorative, opening when ripe to reveal flat, smooth seeds.

BLUE FLAG (*I. versicolor*) is a native of North America, although cultivated versions grow widely in Europe in wetland areas. It has elegant, sword-shaped green leaves lined with shiny silver-gray, and clear blue flower heads with a yellow splash at the throat. Add a few flower heads to potpourri—they are best preserved by drying in a microwave.

JUNIPERUS COMMUNIS
JUNIPER
This coniferous shrub, which grows to 20in-20ft (50cm-6m) tall, produces berries which are used in the production of gin. They are also sold in jars and although dried, appear to be rather soft. Their scent is reminiscent of Christmas, so they are good to use for the center of a festive table arrangement.

LAURUS NOBILIS
BAY
Bay trees will grow to 30ft (9m) tall, although in the wild in Greece they can grow up to 60ft (18m). Known as sweet bay and laurel, it was the Greeks who first gave wreaths of bay leaves to the victors at the Pythian games in Delphi, a custom later adopted by Roman generals. Indeed, the term "bachelor" (of arts, etc.) is probably a derivation of the French *bachelier* or laurel berry. Used in their fresh form, the dark green, shiny leaves are very tough and malleable, and can be easily pinned or glued to florist's foam spheres, baskets, or candles. They can be left to dry and they maintain their color well. They may also be sewn onto fabric. The leaves are highly aromatic and useful in sachets.

LAVANDULA
LAVENDER (L. angustifolia)
This shrubby, highly aromatic plant grows wild throughout southern Europe and is cultivated in North America. It grows to 18in-3ft (45cm-1m) tall and has pretty blue flowers borne on slender gray-green stems. With its fresh, clean scent and charming appearance, it is a versatile herb, frequently used in both aromatic and purely decorative projects.

Although essential oil of lavender is only present in the flower head, the whole plant has a strong scent. This makes it excellent value because the less attractive stems and leaves can be chopped up and used to perfume sachets and pillows where the contents are not seen. Bunches of lavender can be used in a wide variety of projects, including wreaths, wall hangings, tussie-mussies, garlanded baskets, and flowering herb pots.

L. A. 'HIDCOTE' is my favorite among the 20 or so lavender varieties, and it is the one I grow in my own garden. It makes beautiful compact hedges or clumps and has bright blue flowers. Named after Hidcote Manor in England, it flowers from early summer and retains its wonderful deep-shaded flower color even when dried. These flowers are best reserved purely for use in projects where their beauty may be seen; this variety is especially useful for making lavender bundles.

FRENCH LAVENDER (*L. stoechas*) is one of the most beautiful lavender species, with its compact habit, but it is half-hardy. It does not flourish in the open in colder climates, although it does grow wild in the mountains of Spain and France. Its purple flowers and gray-green leaves and stems contain more essential oil than other lavenders.

LIATRIS SPICATA
GAY FEATHER, BLAZING STAR
This perennial, originating from the North American prairies, was introduced into Europe in the the early 1700s. It is unusual because its pink flowers open down the stem, as opposed to the normal practice of opening from the base of the stem up. It is available almost all year round as a cut flower from florists. Garden cultivars grow to 5ft (1.5m) tall and flower from midsummer right through to the end of fall. The flowers make a colorful addition to tussie-mussies, herb wreaths, and flower waters.

LONICERA JAPONICA
HONEYSUCKLE
Many of the honeysuckles are shrubs, grown for their screening qualities. Others are climbers, such as the popular *L. japonica*, one of the most fragrant flowers and a great asset to gardeners wishing to cover an arbor or wall—it can grow to 30ft (10m). Its flowers are creamy white to yellow and tinged with red. They are small but elegantly shaped and look good added to potpourri. *Caution:* the bright red berries that follow the flowers are poisonous.

LUNARIA ANNUA
HONESTY
This plant grows to a height of 36in (90cm). Purple flowers are borne on hairy-stemmed plants which have mauve-gray leaves. The seed pods are flat and oval in shape, with a deep green outer case. Once removed, the flat black seeds are revealed, attached to a fine, silvery-white, tissue-like membrane. These seeds germinate easily and the plant can become invasive. The seed pods may be collected and preserved by the air-drying method. They look good added to potpourri or wired into wreaths and garlands.

MELISSA OFFICINALIS
LEMON BALM, SWEET BALM
Slightly hairy, bright green leaves are borne on square-sectioned stems, which grow to a height of 3ft (1m) to form really large, attractive clumps throughout a border. The leaves smell and taste strongly of lemon when crushed. Bees love its small, creamy-white flowers, which appear throughout the summer. It can be used as foliage in a flower decoration. Dried, it looks less attractive, but once crushed may be used in bath sachets, potpourri, or scented pillows and bags.

MENTHA

SPEARMINT (M. *spicata* 'Moroccan')
Fresh and invigorating, this is the most common of all cultivated mints. It grows to 16in (40cm) tall and, if planted in the open, its roots should be confined in a bucket or pot sunk into the ground, otherwise it will rapidly take over and choke nearby plants. The leaves and flowers look beautiful included in tussie-mussies and are useful when air-dried—add them to bath bags and gentlemen's sachets, and to give a fresh accent to potpourri.

PENNYROYAL (M. *pulegium*) was believed by the Romans to drive away fleas, and many herbalists held it in high regard for treating all kinds of conditions. In some parts of Europe it is still used for culinary purposes, owing to its strong and slightly pungent aroma. This makes it suitable for adding to bath bags and sachets, along with potpourri and also refreshing soaps. It is a dwarf variety of mint, growing to 6in (15cm).

BLACK PEPPERMINT (M. x *piperita*), so named for its purple-tipped leaves, is very vigorous with roots that will rapidly take over a flower bed or container. Growing to a height of 30in (75cm), it has delicate purple-pink flower spikes—wonderful when used as cut flowers in a tussie-mussie or fresh herb wreath. These are easily preserved by air-drying in small bunches.

M. x *VILLOSA* is the variety of mint which grew in the garden of my family home, and it is still one of my favorites. The leaves are rather large and fairly hairy, and have a fresh, clean scent of apples and spearmint. It grows to a height of 3ft (1m) and has soft, fluffy, pink flower spikes. The same planting advice applies to this variety of mint—it is as invasive as the others.

LAVENDER BUNDLES
Bundles of L.a. 'Hidcote' can be laid out to dry on a pretty cloth or tucked into a drawer to scent linen (see pp. 64-67).

MONARDA DIDYMA

BEE BALM, BERGAMOT
Adored by gardeners as well as bees, this plant has become a great favorite owing to its scarlet-red flowers and its lovely aromatic scent. It is used to flavor teas (such as Earl Grey) and is known as "bergamot" because the scent is similar to the Italian bergamot orange. Use it as a fresh herb in tied posies and herb pots, and also when dry because it retains its aroma well. It grows to 24in-3ft (60cm-1m) tall.

MYRRHIS ODORATA

SWEET CICELY
This European native grows almost everywhere that it can find a damp and wooded hollow. Growing to a height of 3ft (1m), it looks similar to Queen Anne's lace and has the same fluffy, green foliage and white, flat-headed flowers borne on hollow stems. Its leaves smell slightly of aniseed and it has shiny black seeds, which were once used to polish wooden floors. It has many culinary uses (its seeds, leaves, and roots are edible) and it is therefore an appropriate addition to a table centerpiece.

MYRTUS COMMUNIS

MYRTLE
This is an evergreen shrub which grows to 8-10ft (2.4-3m) tall and has aromatic leaves and pretty, waxy cream flowers during the late summer months. It was considered sacred to the Greek goddess Aphrodite, and was a traditional ingredient in bridal bouquets for hundreds of years. It is said that a sprig of myrtle cut from a bush grown from the piece included in Queen Victoria's bridal bouquet has been contained in the bouquets of each royal bride ever since. Use the herb in fresh arrangements, such as flowery herb wreaths, as it does not dry well.

117

ROSEMARY POMANDERS

These pomanders can be used decoratively and to scent linen (see pp.46-47). Neatly clipped rosemary spheres make an unusual and interesting arrangement in a polished bowl.

ORIGANUM VULGARE

OREGANO, MARJORAM, *Origanum* comes from two Greek words meaning "mountain joy," because of the cheerful color this herb displays on the hillsides where it grows wild. It will not always survive a harsh winter, however. It grows to 24in (60cm) tall and has lovely purple stems and bright, slightly hairy leaves. In the summer months it has purple-pink flowers and it may be harvested as soon as these are open. With its sweet spicy smell, oregano is a popular decorative herb. Air-dry in small bunches and use in wreaths and posies— its strong stems are easily wired.

PAEONIA OFFICINALIS

PEONY
Superstitions surround this plant. It was once thought to be of divine origin, a protector of shepherds and sheep, and that the root should only be handled on the end of a length of string! Once they are established, peonies will grow to 24-28in (60-70cm) tall and produce flamboyant flowers in many colors. The flowers are easily dried using either the air-drying or silica-gel methods and look wonderful in wreaths and garlands or in potpourri.

PELARGONIUM

SCENTED GERANIUM
These plants are related to true geraniums and are grown for their perfumed and often patterned leaves—the flowers are generally small but the plant itself is bushy and grows to a height of 1-3ft (30cm-1m). They originate from southern Africa and are not frosthardy, though cultivated varieties have been a European favorite since

NIGELLA

LOVE-IN-A-MIST (*N. damascena*) is one of several nigella varieties that are popular with flower arrangers. It grows to 20in (50cm) tall and is indigenous to the Mediterranean area. It is easy to grow from seed and once established will re-seed itself each year. Elegant, soft blue flowers are followed by the hairy seed cases that form a major part of its attraction. The seed cases are large, swollen capsules often marked with purple stripes, and the seeds contained within are small, black, and shiny. Air-dried, both flowers and seed cases are wonderful used in garlands, or fresh in tussie-mussies.

FENNEL FLOWER (*N. sativa*) is closely related to *N. damascena* but bears paler blue to nearly white flowers. Easy to grow from seeds, it is a native of the Mediterranean. The name "nigella" is derived from the Latin for "black," and refers to the shiny black seeds, which were once used as a substitute for pepper. Harvest and air-dry while some of its flowers are not fully matured—this allows some of the petals to be retained in addition to the interesting, fluffy seed heads.

OCIMUM BASILICUM

BASIL
Known also as sweet basil, this herb is found growing wild in tropical and subtropical areas of the world, though it is widely cultivated. The herb grows to 18in (45cm) tall and has soft, green leaves, almost fleshy and very smooth to touch, and small, slightly insignificant white flowers. Basil can be grown indoors, on a windowsill, or outside during the summer. It can be planted in terracotta pots, but must be well watered or the leaves wilt. In ancient Rome it was a sign of love, while in ancient Greece it was a sign of mourning. In India it is a sacred plant for Hindus and considered a protecting spirit of the family and home. A favorite ingredient in Italian and French cuisine, it is the main ingredient in the classic Italian pesto sauce, and is wonderful torn up in salads, especially with tomatoes, or in pasta. Because of its culinary attributes, it makes a vital part of an edible table decoration. The dried leaves are not attractive and should be added to sachets where the contents are hidden.

the late 1600s. They can be planted in containers with other flowering plants. The fresh leaves are wonderful scented ingredients for tussie-mussies and tied posies, or dry them for use in bath bags, scented pillows, and sachets.

PETROSELINUM CRISPUM
PARSLEY

Possibly the most widely cultivated and used of all herbs, its curly, fresh green leaves and clean, distinctive taste and scent have meant continued popularity. It is surrounded by myth and superstition, and the herb has been, rather surprisingly, associated with death and the Devil. Parsley grows to 15in (38cm) tall and its textured leaves are useful in sculptural arrangements. It also makes another vital ingredient in edible table centerpieces.

ROSA
APOTHECARY'S ROSE (*R. gallica*)

Thought to have been first cultivated in the Persian Gulf, the Greeks transported roses with them to Italy and thus they spread throughout Europe. *Rosa* comes from the Greek word for red, "rodon," implying that initial varieties were limited to that shade. It was also grown widely in ancient Rome and Roman brides wore headdresses made of the flowers. Today the rose is the most popular garden plant and the oldest variety is probably *R. gallica*, which reaches 36in (90cm). Use the flower buds and open flower heads in herb wreaths and posies.
DOG ROSE (*R. canina*) has almost no scent but the rose hips, which were used as an ingredient in cough syrup, look lovely added to a potpourri or, when wired in small bunches, to a wreath. This variety usually grows wild to a height of 10ft (3m).
DAMASK ROSE (*R. x damascena*) is one of the most highly scented of all roses. Growing to 6ft (2m) tall, it is cultivated in parts of India

and the East for the perfume industry, where its flowers are gathered and distilled to extract its essential oil. The Mogul emperors made rose oil by steeping the flower heads in oil and pressing the mixture to extract the scent. Use this variety of rose in flower waters.

ROSMARINUS OFFICINALIS
ROSEMARY

A shrubby evergreen plant, with pale blue flowers, rosemary grows to 3-6ft (1-2m) tall and is easily cultivated from a small sprig pushed into dryish soil. Ancient civilizations believed that rosemary could strengthen the memory, and it has long been regarded as a sign of both fidelity and remembrance. Anne of Cleves wore a wreath of it at her wedding to Henry VIII, and her guests were each given a sprig of the herb, gilded and tied with silk ribbon. Grown for its aromatic leaves and culinary uses, it can be planted in the garden or a windowbox, where it provides a supply of fresh materials throughout the year. One of the most versatile herbs, rosemary can be used fresh or dried in most decorative projects.

RUTA GRAVEOLENS
RUE

A native of southern Europe, this is a hardy evergreen which can grow to 24in (60cm) tall. The variety 'Jackman's Blue' has the most wonderful blue-green waxy foliage, bright yellow flowers, and a pungent aroma. Used by the ancient Romans, it is in fact one of the oldest medicinal herbs. Use it purely as a decorative fresh herb. Once dried, it has a more pungent, rather unpleasant smell, making it unsuitable for potpourri. *Caution:* Rue should never be consumed because it is poisonous. Make sure you keep it away from children and pets.

SALVIA OFFICINALIS
SAGE

A Mediterranean native, sage was well-established in English herb gardens by 1600. The genus is huge, with widely varying plants and flower color. *Salvia officinalis* is my favourite, with its purple flowers and furry, gray-silver leaves. The plant grows to a height of 12-30in (30-75cm) and has a strong scent and a warm, almost astringent taste. Arrange sprigs when fresh—once dried the flowers hold their shape perfectly, while the leaves curl slightly. I always try to have a few bunches at hand when making dried herb hangings for the kitchen.
BIENNIAL CLARY (*S. sclarea*) is known in France as *toute bonne* for its medicinal powers. Its soft green, slightly wrinkled leaves turn shades of pinkish-purple with deeper colored bracts and blue flowers. It can grow to a height of 3ft (1m). Gather quantities to use in fresh herb wreaths or as dried material in posies and potpourri. With its vague lavender scent, it works well in soap.

SAMBUCUS NIGRA
ELDER

The elder has frothy white flower heads and is a bushy shrub, growing to 20ft (6m) tall. The flowers make a delicious cordial drink if gathered and steeped with water and sugar, and its berries are sometimes used in wine-making. Although most parts of this elder are used, some species of elder have poisonous parts. The stems are filled with a white pith that is easily removed, leaving hollow pipes, which the Anglo-Saxons used to blow their fires with. The flowers have a very fruity scent and may be dried for use in scented pillows and sachets, or added to potpourri.

SANGUISORBA MINOR
SALAD BURNET

This plant, from the same family as lady's mantle (*Alchemilla mollis*), is also known as garden burnet. It grows to a height of 6ft (2m) and has deep green leaves, which taste similar to borage. It makes an attractive edging to flower beds, with its tall, strong stems and small purple-brown flowers, which look like cattails or enlarged lavender buds. A good foliage plant, it is useful in garlands and herb wreaths; it also makes a tasty addition to soups and salads and is therefore suitable for edible table centerpieces.

SANTOLINA CHAMAECYPARISSUS
LAVENDER COTTON

This is not a member of the lavender family, although its foliage and stem may well be the reason it was so named. An aromatic evergreen, it is wonderful in the garden and looks great planted as part of a knot garden, as a substitute to boxwood. It grows to 20in (50cm) tall, and has silvery-green leaves and tight, yellow, button-like flowers. Pick fresh to use in an arrangement of fresh herbs. It dries well and, being aromatic, is ideal to use in sachets and potpourri.

SATUREJA MONTANA
WINTER SAVORY

This herb is semihardy, with tough woody stems at its base, and is covered in slender, aromatic, dark green leaves. It grows to 15in (38cm) tall and likes fairly poor soils. Once established, the herb makes a good edging plant for borders in an herb garden. It has purple-blue flowers in midsummer, and may be dried at this stage for use in sachets and garlands.

SOLIDAGO
GOLDENROD

Named from the Latin "solidare," meaning "to join," because of its use in healing wounds, this plant is an absolute treasure in the garden, although it is often found growing wild. Growing to 24in (60cm) tall, it is easily established. Tall spikes of bright yellow flowers appear throughout the summer and into the fall. It is also available as a cut flower from florists all year round. Formerly used for dying fabric, it may be air-dried and can be used in all sorts of garlands and posies. Picked fresh, it is an ideal choice for use in a fresh flowering herb pot.

TAGETES PATULA
FRENCH MARIGOLD

Despite its name, this annual originated in the tropics. These flowers grow in fields in India, where they are also an important part of religious ceremonies. A garland of bright orange marigold flowers is presented as a sign of welcome and respect to visitors and elders. Their scent is very pungent and, if grown among other plants in a greenhouse or vegetable patch, helps to discourage greenfly and other pests. French marigold grows to 12in (30cm) tall, and the plant prefers a well-drained fertile soil, but will tolerate dry conditions. Some varieties of this marigold have bicolored flowers. The flowers may be air-dried, although they are best preserved in silica-gel crystals. Their attractive, colorful appearance enhances fresh arrangements, such as tussie-mussies, flowering herb pots, and herb wreaths, as well as dried decorations, including brightly colored potpourri mixtures.

TANACETUM

FEVERFEW (*T. parthenium*), along with its relative *T. balsamita* (commonly known as alecost, bible flower, or costmary), is a beautiful addition to the herb garden. Growing to 36in (90cm), these are easy plants to establish in pots or directly in the ground. They produce small daisy flowers, with golden centers and white petals, throughout the summer. The flowers have a fairly pungent aroma, and look very pretty wired in bunches in a flowery wreath or, once dried, in potpourri, garlands, or swags.
TANSY (*T. vulgare*) may be seen growing wild to 24-36in(60-90cm). Introduced to North America by early settlers, it is widely naturalized. Its strong stem has fluffy, green-frilled leaves, and the flowers are bright yellow buttons, in flat clusters. It has a strong, refreshing scent and is easily air-dried. It is an ideal choice for a flowering pot, and its flower heads look great added to potpourri.

THYMUS VULGARIS
THYME

The pungent garden thymes originated with the wild plant of Asia Minor and the Mediterranean (*T. serpyllum* is a straggly wild thyme known as mother-of-thyme and naturalized in North America). Thyme has a wonderful warm scent and taste, with small purplish flowers that are as effective as lavender in keeping linens free from pests. Growing to 8-38cm (3-15in) tall, it will thrive in almost any tiny crevice, such as between paving stones in a path. Folklore says that fairies like to play among thyme, and Shakespeare refers to it as the abode of the Fairy Queen. A favorite decorative herb, thyme is an excellent fresh material to use in arrangements. When dried, it becomes rather brittle, so use it as a potpourri ingredient. However, a whole sprig or bunch hung where it will not be knocked will last longer. LEMON THYME (*T. x citriodorus*) is another plant perfect for growing either in a pot or between the paving stones of a path, smelling wonderful when stepped on underfoot and standing up to such treatment quite well. This is a slightly smaller variety, growing to a height of 12in (30cm). The herb smells exactly like lemons and the scent is wonderful in soap-making and bath sachets.

VALERIANA OFFICINALIS

VALERIAN

This plant, growing to 24in-5ft (60cm-1.5m) tall, seems able to thrive in the most unlikely places, including dry stone walls and cliffs. It has spires of soft pink or white flowers which, together with its leaves and stems, have an odd scent—some cats find this almost irresistible. It is excellent in the garden, if you can keep the cats away from it. Its roots were used in the Middle Ages, laid among linens and clothes to perfume them, and its oil has been used in soap-making. Today it is used by herbalists to aid sleep.

VERBENA OFFICINALIS

VERVAIN

This perennial has a woody square-sectioned stem, with small pale lilac flowers. Reaching a height of 24in-3ft (60cm-1m), it has been grown for years for its medicinal benefits. Legend says that it was found growing on the Mount of Calvary, where it was used to staunch the wounds of

THYME-WRAPPED CANDLE
Soften the appearance of a plain candle with this simple technique—cover its base with bunches of fresh thyme and secure with jute (see pp.48-49).

Christ. As a result of this, it has been regarded as a highly virtuous herb. It has no scent, but is interesting as an herb garden plant and may be air-dried for using in garlands and swags, or to add visual appeal to potpourri.

VIOLA ODORATA

SWEET VIOLET

This plant grows wild throughout North America but is also a favorite for planting in gardens. It grows to 8in (20cm) tall and has fresh green, heart-shaped leaves, with sweetly scented flowers of a deep purple. Used in the preparation of confectionery and other foods, it was a great

favorite of Queen Victoria's and is grown in vast quantities to supply both florists and the perfumery trade. If steeped in water it will impart its color, so is ideal for inclusion in any floral and herbal waters. It may be air-dried for use in sachets and bags, but to preserve the flowers in a more attractive state, they should be dried using silica-gel crystals. HEARTSEASE (*V. tricolor*) is romantically named and is one of the principal flowers in the love charms used in Shakespeare's *A Midsummer Night's Dream*. Also known as johnny-jump-up, wild pansy, or "three-faces-under-a-hood," its pretty flower heads appear to have faces painted on them. Most garden pansies originate from this plant. The flowers are usually blue or purple mixed with lighter shades and are seen throughout summer and into fall. It is a small plant and grows to a height of 3-5in (8-12cm). Its flowers may be pressed or preserved in silica gel and look charming when added to the top of a bowl of potpourri.

DECORATIVE SPICES

A selection of spices, suitable for decorative purposes, are detailed below. They are listed alphabetically by Latin name, with their familiar common names beneath. The illustrations show the plants and the fruits, seeds, and roots which are used in the projects.

CAPSICUM ANNUUM
CHILI PEPPER

Capsicum, from the Greek word "to bite" refers to the hot, pungent nature of these shiny red and green pods. Christopher Columbus' physician, on board the Santa Maria in the late fifteenth century, mentioned having seen them in the Americas. They were also introduced to India and Africa by the Portuguese. The plant grows to 12in (30cm) tall and the fruit can be up to 6in (15cm) long. The shiny pods are traditionally used for culinary purposes, but they also look beautiful when used in various decorations, such as kitchen wall hangings and centerpieces. However, they must be handled with extreme care, and preferably with rubber gloves (the seeds are the hottest part). *Caution:* Never place chilies within reach of children or pets.

CARUM CARVI
CARAWAY

This plant, which grows to a height of 24in (60cm), was used in the Middle East for thousands of years before its introduction to Europe in the 13th century. It is grown for its seeds, which are used as a flavoring in the making of breads and cakes and cooking in general—a caraway seed cake is an old-fashioned English tea-time favorite. Considered to have a calming effect, caraway seeds make good additions to sleep pillows and scented sachets.

CINNAMOMUM VERUM
CINNAMON

An evergreen, native to eastern and central Asia, Australia and Japan, with other species found in India and China, this is one of the most important of all spice plants. Indeed, the Portuguese invaded Ceylon in 1536 in order to gain the monopoly on its supply. The plant itself grows to 70ft (20m) but the part used is the bark, which has a fragrant taste, and this is generally sold in pieces approximately 3in (10cm) long. The inner layers of the younger tips of bark are the most highly prized. Use small pieces whole in potpourri, crushed among other herbs and spices in sachets and scented pillows, and powdered for soaps.

CROCUS SATIVUS
SAFFRON

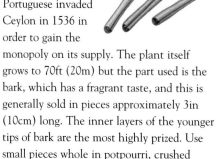

The orange stigmas of this purple-flowered crocus are gathered and dried, and used to flavor and color food and also to dye fabric a rich yellow. This is one of the most expensive spices in the world, with the equivalent of 4,500 flowers being required to yield 1oz (30g) of saffron. This plant, which grows to only 2in (5cm) tall, originated in the Far East and was brought to the Mediterranean and other parts of Europe many centuries ago. Saffron is primarily cultivated in France, Spain, Italy, and Iran.

CUMINUM CYMINUM
CUMIN

This spice plant was indigenous to Egypt, the Mediterranean, and central Asia, and was a favorite condiment among the ancient Greeks. The plant grows to 12in (30cm), but its seeds are tiny. Although the seeds look and smell a little like caraway, it is quite different, and cooks claim it cannot be used interchangeably. Use in robustly scented sachets and potpourris.

CYMBOPOGON CITRATUS
LEMON GRASS

Largely cultivated in the tropical parts of India and Eurasia, lemon grass was initially grown for its oils for use in the perfume industry, when it superseded lemon verbena (*Aloysia triphylla*). The plant can grow to 5ft (1.5m) tall, but the lower part (available in gourmet supermarkets or Oriental specialty markets) is approximately 6in (15cm) in length. Use dry or fresh in sculptural or scented projects.

ELETTARIA CARDAMOMUM
CARDAMOM

These tiny, triangular pale green pods contain highly aromatic seeds, much-used in India in confectionery and *kulfi* (ice cream), and offered together with cumin and caraway seeds at the end of a meal to sweeten the breath. They are a lovely addition to potpourri and sachets, and can also be used in soaps.

ILLICIUM VERUM
STAR ANISE

Growing to 60ft (18m) tall, this is a popular tree in the East, in China and especially Japan, where it is planted near tombs and temples. It is called star anise because of its dark brown, star-shaped seed pods, which are about 1in (3cm) across. These pods look wonderful placed in potpourri and wired into wreaths and garlands. Star anise is available from Oriental specialty markets and supermarkets, and is a popular ingredient in Chinese dishes.

MYRISTICA FRAGRANS
MACE, NUTMEG

Mace is the dried aril of the nutmeg, which surrounds the seed within a fleshy case. In its fresh form it is bright red, and dries to a warm orange-yellow. It is quite brittle and has an identical flavor to nutmeg. It can be bought from supermarkets and is used dried in sachet and potpourri mixtures.

PIMENTO OFFICINALE
ALLSPICE

Also known as Jamaica pepper, this spice is generally known as allspice for its characteristic taste and smell, which is similar to a combination of cloves, pepper, cinnamon, and juniper berries. The crushed berries, which resemble large black peppercorns, are excellent for giving a robust fragrance. It is ideal for use in potpourri or added to gentlemen's sachets.

POGOSTEMON
PATCHOULI

One of the most distinctive of aromas, and very characteristic of India, this highly fragrant shrub is grown there and in Malaysia. The plant grows to 3ft (1m) and its

leaves are cut twice a year and packed into bales. These are then distilled to release the oils, which are used in soaps and perfumes. Some people consider the scent to be too strong, but it can be used sparingly or in a diluted form, which makes it less potent.

SYZYGIUM AROMATICUM
CLOVES

Produced from the dried flower buds of this evergreen tree, which appears as a native plant in Australia, Africa, and Asia, cloves contain large quantities of essential oil. This oil is much used in medicines and perfumes. In China, it was a custom to hold a clove in the mouth to sweeten the breath while addressing the Emperor, and cloves or oil of cloves have been used as a treatment for mild toothache.

Approximately 1/2in (1.2cm) in length, they are essential when making pomanders and give a wonderful, long-lasting aroma if added to potpourri and soaps.

ZINGIBER OFFICINALE
GINGER

A native of Asia, this plant was highly prized among plant collectors in the 19th century, when it was a popular greenhouse and conservatory plant. Much of it now comes from Jamaica and the West Indies. The root, which can be as long as 12in (30cm), is available dried and fresh, and has a wonderful warming aroma and taste. In its fresh form it is very fibrous, but cuts easily into slices, which may be dried and added to potpourri. It adds a warm accent to soaps and flower waters.

HERB-WRAPPED GLASSES
Lemon grass (Cymbopogon citratus) looks wonderful wrapped around glasses (see pp.28-29). Its unusual coloring is set off by the natural tones of this desk arrangement.

BIBLIOGRAPHY/SUPPLIERS

Jeanne D'Andrea. *Ancient Herbs in the J. Paul Getty Museum Gardens.* Malibu, California, 1982.

William, Betsy. *Potpourri and Fragrant Crafts.* Pleasantville, New York, 1996.

Jacqueline Heriteau. *Potpourris and Other Fragrant Delights.* New York, 1973.

Penelope Hobhouse. *Plants in Garden History.* London, 1992.

Mrs M. Grieve FRHS. *A Modern Herbal.* London, 1931.

Christopher Brickell. *RHS Gardeners Encylopedia of Plants and Flowers.* London, 1989.

Deni Bown. *RHS Encyclopedia of Herbs & Their Uses.* London, 1995.

Kathi Keville. *Herbs, An Illustrated Encyclopedia.* New York, 1995.

Barbara Milo Ohrbach. *The Scented Room.* New York, 1986.

Many of the materials used in the projects can be found around the home, or from good art and craft stores, garden centers and malls.

UNITED STATES:
Alloway Gardens and Herb Farm
456 Mud College Road
Littlestown, PA 17340
(717) 359-4548
lavenders (a specialty)

Frontier Natural Products Coop
3021 78th Street
Norway, IA 52318
(800) 669-3275
botanicals, oils, craft supplies

Gilberties Herb Gardens
7 Sylvan Lane
Westport, CT 06880
(203) 227-4175
oils, fresh and dried herbs

Green Valley Flowers & Herbs
1191 North Green Valley Road
Cambria, CA 93428
(805) 927-1368 (fax)
botanicals, oils, fresh-cut herbs, freeze-dried flowers

Lavender Lane
7337 Roseville Road #1,
Sacramento, CA 95842
(888) 593-4400 (toll-free); (916) 339-0842 (fax)
bottles, oils

Lewis Mountain Herbs & Everlastings
2345 S.R. 247,
Manchester, OH 45144
(937) 549-2484; (937) 549-2886 (fax)
botanicals, freeze-dried roses (a specialty), dried herbal and everlasting plants

Penzeys Ltd.
PO Box 933 , Muskego, WI 53150
(414) 679-7207
spices and other botanicals

Shady Acres Herb Farm
7815 Highway 212
Chaska, MN 55318
(612) 466-3391; (612) 466-4739 (fax)
oils, botanicals, fixatives

CANADA:
Happy Valley Herbs
3505 Happy Valley Road,
Victoria, BC V9C 2Y2
(250) 474-5767
botanicals, lavender (a specialty)

Magnolia's
Box 220
Zephyr, ON L0E 1T0
(905) 473-1672
botanicals, oils

Richter's
357 Highway 47
Goodwood, ON L0C 1A0
(905) 640-6677; (905) 640-6641 (fax)
botanicals, oils, plants

Stewart's Touch of Nature
PO Box 91
Petersburg, ON N0B 2H0
(519) 634-5594
oils, herbs, containers

Trouvez
2237 Chemin des Patriotes
Richelieu, QC J3L 4AZ
(514) 658-7311
botanicals, oils, roses (a specialty)

INDEX